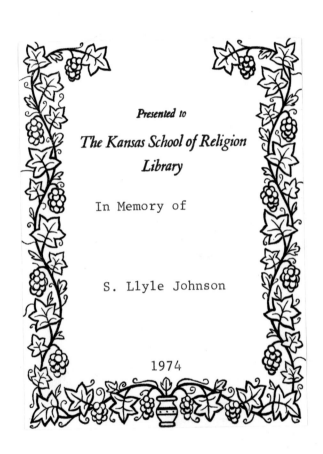

Presented to

The Kansas School of Religion
Library

In Memory of

S. Llyle Johnson

1974

The Religious Press
in America

The

MARTIN E. MARTY

Religious

JOHN G. DEEDY, JR.

Press

DAVID WOLF SILVERMAN

in

ROBERT LEKACHMAN

America

GREENWOOD PRESS, PUBLISHERS
WESTPORT, CONNECTICUT

The Library of Congress has catalogued this publication as follows:

Library of Congress Cataloging in Publication Data
Main entry under title:

The Religious press in America.

    1. Journalism, Religious. I. Marty, Martin E.,
1928-
[PN4888.R4R4 1972]   070.4'82'0973   72-6844
ISBN 0-8371-6500-8

Originally published in 1963
by Holt, Rinehart and Winston, New York

This edition is published by arrangement
with Holt, Rinehart and Winston, Inc.

First Greenwood Reprinting 1972

Library of Congress Catalogue Card Number 72-6844

ISBN 0-8371-6500-8

Printed in the United States of America

Contents

Preface

A SUSTAINED analysis of the religious press in America has long been overdue. Despite the undoubted size of the enterprise—figures are not thoroughly reliable, but a total circulation of 50,000,000 has been estimated—for most of us it is a largely invisible phenomenon. The person who subscribes to a denominational publication is rarely familiar with the range of newspapers and magazines which claim to interpret the world in terms of his religious commitment, to say nothing of other faiths. As for the general public, it has little way of knowing the amount of influence such journals have, or what kind of influence it may be.

The editors who have contributed essays to this volume—Martin E. Marty, John G. Deedy, Jr., and David Wolf Silverman—are thoughtful and influential representatives of journalism within the American Protestant, Catholic, and Jewish communities. They not only provide some much-needed historical perspective for the different branches of American religious journalism, but deal with basic and difficult questions: What is the audience for such publications, and what are its special interests and presuppositions? What is the nature of "news" in the religious press? How good a job is this press doing? What factors tend to blunt its impact and prevent it from better achieving its basic purpose?

Both descriptive material and prescriptive analysis are provided. In the process our essayists offer balanced and provocative remarks on the religious interpretation of political situations and on the delicate problem of handling public issues which tend to divide Americans along religious lines. Their criticism is mostly positive, and many of their suggestions offer fruitful possibilities, but they are unanimous in criticizing the way in which key issues of religious concern are often either ignored or made to appear trivial.

The book concludes with a commentary on these essays by an informed outsider to the world of religious journalism. Robert Lekachman voices the sympathetic concern of the secular community that the religious press do more to inform the public of the relevance of its various religious traditions to the problems we share in common, and reminds church-related editors that they must perform their task in the light of the same high standards that they invoke in commenting on the secular community.

The Religious Press

in America

1 The Protestant Press:

LIMITATIONS AND POSSIBILITIES

MARTIN E. MARTY

THE Associated Church Press, an organization which includes most of the more important Protestant magazine publishers, was meeting in New York in the spring of 1962. One of the editors present, Dr. G. Elson Ruff of *The Lutheran,* told an anecdote to prove his point in a panel discussion. The anecdote (no doubt fictional, we hope) referred to life in one of the newly merging Protestant denominations. Out of the merger was to grow a new church paper, and the officials were concerned that the paper should receive wide distribution and be read by all.

According to Ruff, they conceived the idea of making support of the paper a matter of conscience for the members of the new Christian group. They would rewrite the book of worship and particularly the ceremony by which new members are received. Customarily, in this ceremony a number of vows are taken. In the rubrics of the new order this line would appear: "And do you solemnly promise that you will faithfully and regularly read our church's official paper?"

The member-to-be responds: "I do so solemnly promise, with the help of Almighty God . . ."

This anecdote, which I hope I have reproduced accurately, since it belongs to the oral tradition, turns out to be a parable. In it are contained many of the main themes that must be reckoned with in any discussion of the press in evangelical Christian circles in North America. The reference to the Associated Church Press indicates that Protestant publishing is a large, ubiquitous, well-organized, and well-promoted venture. The reference to a self-critical, able, and modest editor suggests the presence of an able and qualified leadership. The new denomination's compulsive feeling that its house-organ magazine must be widely disseminated and read is a reminder of the investment of money, hope, and energy by large organizations in the media which they subsidize. The grimness with which reading is placed on the readers' conscience signifies the somewhat humorless purposiveness of denominational life. The quasi-religious cast of the promise to read is not at all untypical of the way in which Protestants tend to mix sacred obligation with the optional and arbitrary elements of group life. Most of all, mention of the necessity for invoking divine aid for the task of getting a magazine read suggests that a roomful of editors (response to Ruff's story was enthusiastic) realize that the Protestant press is in a difficult situation and needs help.

The chief trouble that afflicts Protestant publishing has little to do with fiscal or technical matters. Instead, the uneasiness is due to the disparity that exists between the expectations brought to the religious press and the limits of performance. By performance I mean particularly the problem of the minimum return which the best of editors and writers can produce in the present context of religious publishing.

This disparity, this conflict between expectation and product, is the main theme of this chapter. No doubt many of the problems involved are not unique to Protestantism, but are written into the very process of publishing. Seldom does an organ reach as wide and significant a readership as its producers desire; seldom does it have the hoped-for effect. In the secular press as well as in the religious there are serious limitations of context. There are limits of literacy, limits to what money and time the public will invest, limits of areas of interest which even the motion-picture magazines, the Sunday supplements, or the weekly picture magazines must face. Customer resistance, readers' preconceptions and precommitments—these are problems everywhere.

Our task is merely to discuss the nature of these problems for Protestantism where, paradoxically, they appear to be most intense. Ostensibly it is the most exposed of all religious families; it lives at many edges of national experience. In the past it obviously vivified and informed many significant gestures and modes of thought in the United States. In a slightly more restricted and thoroughly revised way, it still does. The instrument for interpreting this exposed life to the Protestant community, as well as to the larger social and political body, should be the press. The outsider will not become familiar with Protestantism through its pulpit, its private life. The adherent will not find the pulpit the best instrument for relating Protestant witness to the public life; it is chartered to do something else. If the press, therefore, is somehow limited in its primary function, not only the inner life of Protestantism, but in many ways the public life of a nation with a Protestant religious majority will not be well served.

What has been said should help make clear the reason for the existence of this book and this chapter. No one outside the circle of professional publishing need concern himself with most of the problems an Associated Church Press must discuss. The general public can fulfill its various vocations unmindful of the market, of publishing procedures, of editors' ulcers, migraines, and endocrine disturbances. But the general public is involved in the public portrait and the public pretensions of America's large religious groups. That public has a right to examine the *psyche* of the press to determine the seriousness with which various options present themselves as they bid for national attention. It can and should appraise the self-definition with which large institutions in a free society operate. It can raise questions as to whether—even if the technical and marketing aspects of the press are efficient—the Protestant press currently is working with a clear set of intentions.

In addition, interpretation is obviously necessary: Protestants hardly see anything of the Roman Catholic press, and almost never see the Jewish. So, too, Catholics and Jews are hardly mindful of the nature of Protestant publishing; this is largely shrouded from their view. Other religious groups, co-responsible for spiritual life in a free society, deserve a coherent view of Protestant publishing. We may also hope that the informed citizen who is uncommitted to any of the large religious groups will also have a concern about the self-understanding such large forces employ and hold.

IS THERE
A PROTESTANT PRESS?

To this point we have assumed that the reader is aware of the existence and the ubiquity of Protestant publishing efforts. Even this assumption may be misplaced in the face of the non-Protestant reader. He may wonder how we can speak of such powerful, well-supported, consuming ventures in publishing. He may ask a prior question which could set us back: *"Is there a Protestant press?"*

The question must be taken seriously; it is not facetiously spoken or reproduced. Is there a Protestant press? In the public life of the nation the whole venture is well-nigh invisible. Any reader can begin with a simple test of personal experience. If he is not a Protestant: of the Protestant majority of the nation's estimated 1,500 religious periodicals, how many has he himself seen? By how many has he been confronted? How many has he been referred to? How many has he read? The Protestant can take the same test: how many *outside* his denomination (belonging to other denominations, to interdenominational or non-denominational agencies) can he name or has he confronted?

The invisibility and undercover aspect of Protestant publishing is sufficiently paradoxical and problematic to deserve further documentation. Where would one expect to find "the press"? The newsstands would be a good place to begin. Religion is one of the most vital concerns of individuals and social groups in

America; propagating particular religions is one of the first goals of these groups; periodicals are a most effective way of propagating ideas, witness, opinion. One would expect to find some representation of a religious voice on the newsstand. Admit that the limitations of the corner drugstore do not offer too many possibilities for the Protestant press. Go to the newsstand of a large airport or train station, for these are the repositories of most of the popular evidences of our culture. The Protestant press will be invisible; it does not ordinarily present itself in the competitive world of the newsstand. The newsstand certainly gives evidence of the "post-Christian" cultural dimensions of life today. Only when a mass magazine chooses to emphasize religion will it be represented. At this point we are not faulting Protestantism for this absence, nor explaining it, nor resolving the problem, nor dealing with market complexities. Now it is only to be noted.

If one goes to the most comprehensive magazine markets, does the picture differ? Among the thousands of periodicals presented in the largest Chicago outlet, for example, what Protestant evidences are available? *The Christian Century, Christianity and Crisis, Christian Herald, Christian Life,* and *Church Management* were all that were recently on display. They were not conspicuous, nor attractively offered, but they were available to the seeker—in the "C" section under the heading, "Opinion."

The invisibility of the Protestant publishing venture is equally apparent at public libraries. On the national level, ordinarily only some of the magazines just listed will be easily accessible. Regionally, where one denomination is very strong (for example, Southern Baptists in the South), metropolitan libraries may give a significant place to denominational magazines. Elsewhere denominational magazines will usually be merely available. Well-intentioned churches and church members are advised to extend their witness through the public libraries, but the gratis subscriptions which are sent usually end up on the "general" shelf or the "junk" pile. In several recent studies, *The Christian Century* was the only Protestant magazine among the twenty journals most often asked for by readers at public libraries.

If we move from newsstand and library to the level of secondary reference, the Protestant press hardly begins to emerge from obscurity. The literate citizen who reads one or another of the weekly news magazines or major newspapers, the person who receives some of his notions of reality from the Associated Press and the United Press International will be brought into contact with certain elements of the Protestant press. One or two nondenominational journals will be quoted because of their exposure to national life, and because they are not regarded as propagandizers of a particular element within Protestantism. Rarely is a denominational magazine quoted in those portions of the press which are in contact with the larger public. The pattern of invisibility remains.

Even the serious researcher is handicapped in gaining access to the religious press. Few magazines deserve indexing in the *Readers' Guide to Periodical Literature,* so that access must be had to specialized bibliographies. The religious life of America cannot be chronicled without reference to the month-to-month reporting of the magazines which have proliferated since the early nineteenth century. But concerning the life of the journals themselves, their intentions and mechanisms, there had until the recent past been relatively little curiosity. A 1,219-page bibliography of American religion, the most complete to date,[1] is able to devote only two and one-half pages to "Histories of Periodical Literature" (I, 21 f.) and "The Religious Press" (II, 952 f.).

"Writings on the American religious press are far from numerous or satisfactory. To a great extent this field still awaits exploration by secular and church historians." (p. 21)

In the second volume of the bibliography the general disinterest in studies of the religious press is set into a more dramatic context:

[1] Nelson R. Burr, *A Critical Bibliography of Religion in America* (Princeton: Princeton University Press, 1961).

"Obviously, the denominational and independent religious press has had an immense effect upon the national life and thought. It has shaped the opinions of religious and even of other persons [sic], on a broad variety of religious, moral, and general public topics and questions. There are, however, comparatively few publications which examine specifically the influence of the religious press. . . ." (p. 952)

The visibility of the Protestant press to the general public is found to consist of two or three opinion journals placed on metropolitan newsstands and in libraries; secondary references in the news magazines and wire services (usually references to the same magazines); and a very occasional incident related to the personalities or issues of the denominational press. Such a paucity of contact would suggest that the Protestant press is not vital, is comatose. Anything but this is true. Furious activity, competition, zeal, energy, and staggering financial investments are directed toward the publication of religious periodicals. We are dealing, therefore, with a complex situation in the context of American religion, Protestantism, and denominational life.

"Is there a Protestant press?"

If one puts on his denominational spectacles and looks around, he confronts an entirely different scene. Now he becomes aware of a rather scientific attempt to use the press to nurture the private world of the various denominations. Within the limits of this science and along the lines of its functionality, most Protestant editors could make a reasonably good case for their responsibility and their successes. Measured by these private standards of intention and achievement, the church organizations are served as well as they might be expected to be. Certainly Methodism is as well served by *Together* as Rotarians are by *The Rotarian,* and members of the United Church of Christ are better served by the United Church of Christ *Herald* than are Lions by *The Lion* and lionism. The more serious question, however, is this: Is the self-nurture of a denomination through a house organ the highest goal the Protestant press should have?

Space and assignment forbid the introduction of detailed analyses of the Protestant publications. But one may run a finger down the roster of the Associated Church Press Directory and point to various kinds of vitalities and achievements. *The American Lutheran,* listed on the first page of the directory, calls to mind the role of the independents within denominations. For years it has represented a responsible voice as "the loyal opposition" within a conservative Lutheran institution, and any number of its arguments and issues have deserved a wider audience. The *Bible Society Record* each month keeps its nose above church politics and informs 700,000 readers of developments in the fields of literacy, publication, and world Bible distribution.

The *Christian Herald* is a phenomenon all to itself. At present, with an audited circulation of almost 450,000, it is the most successful "mass" magazine in Protestant independent circles. *Christianity and Crisis,* and *Christianity Today* are two of the better-known opinion journals and represent elements of the public dimension which will be discussed later in this chapter.

The polemic side of Protestantism is evidenced in *Church and State Review,* the organ to which 115,000 members of "Protestants and Other Americans United for the Separation of Church and State" subscribe. *The Churchman* is a reminder of a vigorous era of radical social thought within Episcopalianism. *Church Management* is a thoroughly professional, though largely uncritical, review of the administrative side of church life. *Concern* is an attractive biweekly summary of traditional Methodist social concerns—everything from anti-racism to pro-temperance. The *Crusader* is the busiest-looking Protestant magazine, reporting in ample pictorial detail the activities of American Baptist Convention officials. *The Episcopalian* is a sleek, attractive journal which strides a fine line between promoting the institution and nudging it into a world concern. *Eternity* is the finest representative of what once would have been called "Fundamentalist" viewpoint in print. *Greater Works,* an organ of the Brotherhood of the American Lutheran Church, is a model of typographic achievement.

The *International Journal of Religious Education* deserves a place with the best secular journals in its call to religious educators for high levels of competence. *Liberty,* related to Seventh-Day Adventist concerns for separation of church and state, has rallied supporters of the cause beyond the Adventist group; this indicates the trans-denominational, but still intra-Protestant, possibility of common interests present in the press. *The Lutheran* is an always news-filled, often controversial, serious representative of official publishing. *The Lutheran Standard,* like the *United Church Herald,* suggests the potential of the magazines that grow out of merging denominations. Each is greater than the sum of its two previous parts. *The Mennonite* reveals how a small denomination (this one not always regarded as in the Protestant main stream) may set a standard for format, photography, and ethical concern which shames the bloated bigger brothers.

The Methodist Layman often moves away from strictly organizational concerns and presents vital issues, something its feminine counterpart, *The Methodist Woman,* less frequently does. *Motive* is an *avant-garde* Methodist student magazine which, while perhaps overly voguish, certainly reveals an intense preoccupation with the faith in the real world of the intelligentsia. The *Christian Advocate* has and often succeeds in the task biweekly of helping the Methodist ministry move into a new age and find a new self-image. *Presbyterian Life* is typical of the magazines which upgraded themselves from their origins: many considered it to be "conceived in iniquity" as a "slick" representation of middle-class religiousness. Under Robert J. Cadigan, and with salty associates like John R. Fry in the fold, it has broken much of this stereotype, and asserted considerable independence. In an act of courage rare among official journals, *Presbyterian Life* not too long ago editorially advised one of the denomination's wealthiest members and his circle of followers (in the face of criticism of Presbyterian social concerns): The denomination is not for sale. *This Day* is a *Together*-type Lutheran magazine, and *Together* is a *This Day*-type Methodist magazine; each presents, in lusciously technicolor format, the bearing of aspects of the Christian faith on middle-class, semi-rural denominationalism. Each of them has also, in recent years, begun to show a somewhat more serious concern for a world whose problems go beyond those of personal anxiety and fulfillment.

Citing these magazines, sometimes with favor, is not done with the intention of providing an award system (the Protestant press already hands itself more awards than it needs or deserves). It is, rather, to suggest some of the scope of independent as well as official publishing ventures inside Protestantism. It does not distract from the point made earlier concerning the invisibility of this portion of the press: hardly anyone outside the denominations or, occasionally, the interest groups represented, sees any of these periodicals. They are, almost all of them, operating with a clearly defined limit of functionality. This does not mean that their circulations are small. Along the margin of *The Associated Church Press Directory* one is not at all startled to come across circulations of the following amounts: 240,000; 185,000; 365,000; 700,-000; 280,000; 431,000; 335,000; 196,000; 300,000; 1,150,000; 940,-000. While many of these numbers may be "captive audience" under the "blanket subscription" idea, at their worst these statistics represent an enterprise which would cause envy in the minds of many commercial publishers.

Religious institutions have adjusted with acumen to the necessities of a technical society. They know the need to rally and inform and inspire groups of people who are widely separated geographically. Even the smallest groups and the more primitive indicate a real faith in dissemination through the printed word. *The Year Book of the American Churches* is very revealing on this point. The Church of God (Abrahamic Faith) lists 5,300 members and has a periodical biweekly (*The Restitution Herald*). The 301,826 Seventh-Day Adventists are served through twenty-two periodicals, only a few of them regional. The 2,200 American Rescue workers have their *Rescue Herald*. (The 317 General Six-Principle Baptists fail us; they have none.) But the 100 Independent Baptist Church of America members in two congregations have at least a quarterly, *The Lighthouse.* Very few ecological niches are unfilled.

In this skip, hop, and jump over the multitude of evidences of publishing energies, one is inspired to ask what the Protestant press lacks. Near our conclusion we shall suggest one or two future directions that might imply a possible new kind of journal. For the moment, a reader may be curious concerning the absence of a Protestant daily newspaper. Only one publication in America remotely meets such a description and deserves reference here. *The Christian Science Monitor,* one of the most respected newspapers in America, has a religious orientation which is non-Catholic, non-Jewish, and thus, in the public eye, Protestant. Many Christian Scientists are uneasy with the designation, and most other Protestants have difficulty envisioning Christian Science as part of any Protestant family.

Even though the *Monitor* does not belong to the mold, it should be considered here. First, it unashamedly proclaims its denominational orientation, even in its masthead. Second, it is faithful to the denomination, completely—as one would expect in that instance—uncritical of the institution which gives it life. Third, it is slightly restricted in its coverage because of a number of totems which the publishers call attention to, and a number of taboos from which they flee. Well known among these are curiously ambivalent accounts of deaths, and a minimization of the part that tobacco and alcohol play in the world. Fourth, religious propaganda is at a minimum; one editorial is devoted to it on occasion, and that is usually presented inoffensively.

With those preliminaries in mind, the main observation is in order. The *Monitor,* better than any other existing representative of the American religious press, is willing to forgo institutional self-seeking and self-representation for the sake of a service function: gathering, reporting, and interpreting the news responsibly for the larger public. At least this clue, this willingness to make use of religious resources for the good of society, should be recognized as a model of what most Protestant publishers could remember and from which they could learn.

However, many exceptional features, not easily reproducible elsewhere in Protestantism, went into the formation of that religiously founded daily. More important, should Protestantism have a daily? Given the existing state of affairs I would advance an emphatic "No." I am not sure that Protestantism is ready or willing to forgo enough of its own institutional prerogatives and competition to subsidize the only kind of venture that would be worthy. Were it to proceed with existing ecclesiastical goals in mind, the result could be nothing but embarrassing. Not that the public press of the United States is in such good condition that it needs no new competition; rather, new competition from the religious world could not at present be forthcoming. The defensiveness, the concern for the reputation of the denomination, and the attention to petty and trivial details of organizational life scarcely allow hope for a good daily in which Protestants would "go underground" for the sake of the societal need for better news coverage.

If daily newspapers, therefore, will play no further part in this discussion, so neither will the scholarly journals, quarterlies, and purely technical theological publications. In so many respects they are a separate field, with such limited circulations that they belong more to the world in which book publication is to be analyzed; in the public eye they are not "the press." Most of our emphasis will fall on weekly, biweekly, and monthly magazines and newsletters.

The Protestant press is in a paradoxical situation. To the public it is largely invisible. To Protestantism it is furiously active and ever-present. If this is the context, how did it come about; should it have come about; can anything be done, if it is desirable to do anything about it? Another way to put matters is this: the genius of Protestantism demands a lively press. Protestantism conceives of itself as the most exposed religion in the American complex, yet its press is not exposed to the public. By definition, and limited by its current context, it is prevented from serving the larger society and even from being of much aid in presenting the most honest "image" of Protestantism to the non-Protestant. Great expectations are met with minor fulfillments, not because of financial, technical, or personal deficiencies so much as by the setting and definition. The parts are greater than the whole. In the small battles of individual denominations, the press may here and there effect a major victory; in the larger arena, it seems to add to an already trivially regarded religious institutionalism. Reference to this context will do more to inform a public concerning the Protestant press than would a repetitious periodical-by-periodical survey of assets and liabilities.

Why is it, even though technical competence is not lacking, that so much of the activity of the religious institution seems to be halfhearted, low-keyed, beside the point? Why is there so often a humorless, unimaginative drift in relation to the world's dynamisms, especially since religious institutions have considerable dynamic and can gather considerable loyalties? Why do people in the religious press bring such low expectations to each other's products? Bishop Gerald Kennedy defines a sermon as something a minister will cross the country to preach but not cross the street to hear. Similarly, the obsession each denomination has with its own literary product is not carried over into an expectation from another's.

On campuses, in factories or union halls, in art galleries, in centers of communications, and at political meetings, one observes an entirely different kind of world than the one portrayed as important in much of the religious press. To this former world the latter possesses little significance. Religious people are so used to this circumstance that it surprises them to conceive that it could be otherwise. Yet as "power blocs," Protestant and Catholic institutions at least must be reckoned with; they are admired for their efficiency, endeavor, and fund-raising ability. Why is so little expectation brought to what they have to say, to the substance of their proclamation? Is this situation responsible entirely for the overdefined functionality of the Protestant press as it speaks only to certain aspects of institutional life? Does the Protestant press contribute to the situation? At best, could it help extricate the churches from their current cultural estrangement?

Institutional might, and personal loyalty not matched by (in the best sense) ideological strength—this is the public picture of the churches, and it is reflected in most of the intentions of the religious press.

Without romanticizing the past, one is tempted to ask whether the Protestant churches could have come to this position of institutional strength if they had not had some more constructive relation to culture at large in the past. How long can one have the luxury of having "the faith" taken seriously if one is culturally trivial? A reading of the religious press suggests that most editors and most churchmen do have a view of the past which gave them their original charter. Most definition in denominationalism is still determined by nineteenth-century imagery. In that pattern America was a Protestant culture. Laws, mores, ethos, patterns, habits were supposed to be informed by evangelical witness; when the Protestant editor talked to his own flock, he was automatically addressing the culture as such.

He knows that does not happen today. He deals with partial elements of the culture. His audience lives a split-level existence. In the sermon, the Bible class, the religious periodical, "holy" words take on private meanings and minister to only one dimension of life. The other 166 or so hours of a week are spent in a different kind of real world to which the religious words are seldom addressed. For one or two hours a week, if a churchgoer spends them with religious periodicals, he is asked to give as much attention to a fund-raising appeal, the laying of a cornerstone in a distant state, and/or the ordination of a new minister, as he does to a sit-in in the South or a refugee program in an underdeveloped part of the world. Such a distortion of emphasis dislocates his ability to determine what is important in his daily life.

The easiest reaction for any but the most alert Protestant editor to show is one of anger at being left out of important determinations, or regret over the passing parade. This is evident in the pervasive hand-wringing over the "secularism" to which nonreaders of the magazine in question—it is assumed—are wholly committed and to which halfhearted readers are themselves tempted. Instead of seeing the Christian potential in a revolutionary world, page after page of the religious press is devoted to repealing that world. Sometimes this takes the form of denying revolutionary change. The "isms" are useful; they drive people together during a fund-raising appeal. But they are not really so radical that they force reappraisal of the faith in the world. Other periodicals will try to counteract the "isms" by pointing to hitherto unrecognized vitalities in Christianity and specifically in Protestantism.

An aspirant writer who wishes to publish in most Protestant journals would do well to document an article such as: "This is not the post-Christian era," or, "Who says this is not a Protestant culture?" "The Amazing Vitality of Christianity" is the actual title of a piece in *Christianity Today* by an astute and no longer aspirant writer, Kenneth Scott Latourette. In the context of his life work, such references to vitality are well-earned luxuries. For most readers, the signs to which he points add up to something different: a charter not to have to recognize the cultural insignificance of much Christian enterprise. Building one more dike against the seas of "secularism" may have a limited usefulness, but as a major theme—which it seems to be—in religious publishing it is hardly productive. Some of this editorial impulse is, no doubt, the result of a "house-organ" relation to institutions which depend on a misinterpretation of culture. For the most part, the editors are themselves the pace setters in denominational hierarchies; they are more alert than others to the meaning of change because of their involvement in a vocation and a fraternity in which the mass media bring aspects of a revolutionary world to them constantly. But somehow a diminution of energy and vision occurs somewhere between what they personally regard the world to be, and what their final printed product suggests.

One hesitates to take examples; no matter how random the choice, he may seem to be singling out a culprit when he is dealing with a general problem. But the very randomness of choice is actually illustrative. The March 1962 issue of the

Crusader, the American Baptist news magazine, is illustrative. Much can be said in favor of the magazine. It is newsy, it is not dull. It is crammed with illustrations and generally outspoken in viewpoint. But its "real" world consists in telling Baptists about Baptists. A content analysis would reveal the following:

The cover is titled: "Baptist Works on Explorer XII." Scientists can be Christians, too, we are reminded on this cover in the typically defensive posture which first acknowledges the world's patterns of power, and then hitches churchmanship to it. Lewis Paul, a member of the Calvary Baptist Church of Washington, D.C., is pictured working on a space craft. (This was the month after John Glenn's orbital flight.)

Inside cover: two pictures, one of children in a Baptist church in New Hampshire (dressed in Revolutionary War clothes to dramatize the church's contribution to the "Valley Forge Forward Fund"—a denominational program), and another of a Baptist, Elbert E. (Pearly) Gates, leading Robert Kennedy around Hong Kong, set the stage. A fine editorial under the pictures criticizes the busy-busyness of denominational and congregational programming. "About this Issue" informs us—accurately—that it will be "packed with information and pictures of significance to American Baptists." Under this is a report on "Unified Budget Giving" in the denomination during the month. There is also room to report on six studies of the denomination's goals (budget, theological education, administrative areas, conventions, tenure of office, and commissioning of ministers).

Page three is a full-page account of the February sessions of the general council of the denomination, and a report of one of its committees; these certainly represent legitimate reporting in a denominational magazine. The next page is devoted to "Polish Baptists Open Seminary," an event which holds newsworthy interest also beyond religious circles this side of the Iron Curtain. Continuing through the magazine we find a page devoted to a profile: "Meet Dewey Creasman, First Vice President of the American Baptist Convention." He is "as folksy and grass roots a first vice-president as the American Baptist Convention is ever likely to have." (Grass roots are important to editors who smart under the charges of being members of remote bureaucracies.) We learn:

> For more years than he cares to count, Dewey Creasman has rendered yeoman service in Baptist causes. . . . The Creasman theology is conservative, the approach to his fellowmen sanely evangelistic. He is a Republican who votes for Barry Goldwater without subscribing to everything the senator advocates. No radical [sic], Dewey is definitely a man who puts great stock in individual initiative. He fears the encroachment of the welfare state. He has been accused of being anti-ecumenical, but this is a distortion. He finds things both to embrace and to avoid in the National and World Councils of churches. He feels that Baptists should be given the whole story, letting the facts speak for themselves without undue propaganda for or against.

The biographical note is typical of the profile in the denominational press: the man is controversial but not too controversial, opinionated but he does not really want to offend anyone.

An interesting portrait of a Baptist church which gave inspiration to Herman Melville follows for a page and a half; it is accompanied by a reference to Baptist involvement in the Seattle Fair. The two center pages are devoted to Baptist news: four Southern churches welcomed into the Convention; "Montana Convention is Administratively on its Own"; "Michigan Disaffiliates Fountain Street Church"; news items concerning ten Baptists, mostly clergymen, are cited; an executive of the denomination is honored; "Among the churches" reports on Baptist doings; California women are pictured at a Baptist pageant ("Winter Wonderland"). The usual church ground-breaking ceremony, athletes speaking at a church, a new Tokyo chapel, a missionary, a medical doctor who is a missionary, and the *Crusader's* editorial staff are pictured; a report on Baptist higher education rounds out the page.

Following this are two pages which take the most notice of the outside world. Except for a column about ordination standards and Baptist giving, most space is given here to letters concerning a controversial (and largely anti-) United Nations editorial in a previous issue, and to a column of careful reporting on what U.N. affairs mean for Baptists. The next two pages distract from this interest, being given over to pictures of three dozen Baptist leaders. One of them, Edgar J. Goodspeed, deserves more attention than he received. The others are listed among scores of pastoral changes and bureaucratic shuffles. Each is important to a region or a circle of relatives, but the general reader—Baptist or not— is turned away by the plethora of portraits and personalities. The net result is a trivialization of news concerning the significant changes.

A Baptist leader is listed on the following page as bound on a National Council mission to the Soviet, a committee working on the denomination's convention is pictured, and a number of general religious news items surround them. Inside the back cover is related an event in the career of former President Truman's pastor, which is not without human interest; it is accompanied by some words on the relevance of church membership to the scientist pictured on the cover. The last page picks up the theme of the editorial: overworked parsons, of whom too much is expected institutionally. Finally, just to be properly ecumenical, John Glenn is quoted as having "taught Sunday School in the Presbyterian Church," and being on the board of trustees.

At almost every turn in the road the reader is directed to issues of the time: the United Nations, science, astronauts, Presidents, institutionalization, and so on. But the "house-organ" character prevents the editor from undertaking to determine the real significance of any of them, by the fact that he is under the morale-building and loyalty-enhancing compulsion to show that at every crucial turn of life there is someone who belongs to the proper denominational club. The editor might well respond: Do you expect me to do something other than tout the virtues of the denomination that foots the bill? Shouldn't *U.S. News and World Report* cover its world and I cover mine? His implied answer to his kind of question is clear from his choice of subject matter; whether the decision is wise depends upon the criteria with which one approaches the religious press.

If the *Crusader* represents a frustrating and illusory tie-in to the secular world, the March, 1962 issue of *The Methodist Woman* is in a similar relation to the ecumenical world. Again it may be argued that the magazine serves its sponsoring institution well; it is crammed with the part Methodist women play on the world scene. The cover contains a scene from New Delhi and the symbol of the World Council of Churches. (It is to be noted that we are not dealing with the denominational press at its worst, in a polemic, sub-Christian, anti-ecumenical tone—examples of that abound but would raise the wrong issues here; we are dealing with responsible examples of the microcosmic, self-contained, institutional world.)

The Methodist Woman features "Methodist Women at New Delhi," and "The Methodist of the Year," and is filled with reports of organizational finances, missionary arrivals and departures, obituaries, jurisdictional reports, service reports, how-to-do-it advice, travel guides to the annual convention, promotion materials, pledge services, calendars of activities, scholarship opportunities, maps of World Federation of Methodist Women activities, reports from homes for the aged run by the organization, deaconess centers, conference reports, and—we hasten to add—fine reports on community centers, and an excellent study guide on the church's social participation.

This issue is typical of the many organizational magazines which serve their institutions reasonably well. But by the attempt at total coverage of affairs significant and insignificant, they give the reader little guidance concerning what is really important in church life and what is merely administrative detail. They create the impression that installation of officers of a women's circle in New Hampshire should interest an Arizona Methodist women's group in much the same way as the New Delhi ecumenical convention does. In short, where there could be parables there is a welter of confusing detail; where there could be focus on occasional sacrificial lives and institutions there is trivialization by the parity of total coverage. The net result may be the strengthening of certain loyalties to one Christian institution, though even here no doubt some interest is lost in the confusion. At the same time, the total impact of a Protestant witness to the world through the press is limited by the indiscriminate blending of a good magazine, a chatty suburban-type newspaper, and organizational gossip.

One has to be an American Baptist leader to care about news in the *Crusader;* and a leader in a specific organization, with a specific emphasis of a specific denomination, to care about the real world surrounding *The Methodist Woman.* One last insistence: these magazines were chosen not as being bad examples, but as good examples across the spectrum; they were singled out not as culprits but as representatives.

Certainly there must be specialization and specificity. However, in a press that sets out to serve a large clientele (soon almost 90 million Americans over the age of twelve will be ready to list themselves as "Protestant" to the poll-takers), more place must be found than now exists to serve the general and inclusive interest of a generation that is not engrossed in institutional detail and still wants to be Christian. No term better characterizes the emergent Protestant collegiate generation than "anti-institutional," and no attitude is more common within it than impatience with piddling organizational self-preoccupation. Instead of ministering to it, the Protestant press in most instances seems oblivious, and reports on business as usual.

To point to the obsolescence of these concerns is not a popular function, and writing a chapter such as this is hardly the way to promote oneself for a place in Protestant publishing. Yet I have confidence that most editorial boards, given the same assignment of taking an overview of the evangelical press in the national context, would be moved to comment similarly. We are not called to give editors extensive advice and make suggestions about minor revision. It is in place, however, to question the whole context in which the work proceeds.

Since the editors are presumed, indeed known, to know a great deal about the nature of a culture (no longer Protestant) in which they move, and about the disaffection in which religious institutionalism is held, it would seem that their main task is to sustain the imagination to call their two worlds of vocation and understanding together. Could much of the energetic reporting on the time-consuming activities of Protestant institutions be a cover-up for editorial understanding of the insignificance of the whole mission, or is this a failure in communications?

When a honeybee is collecting honey from a flower its abdomen can be removed and the forward end of the bee will go on drawing honey, only to have it discharged into the open air. This is a failure on one part of an animal to take into account what the condition of another part is. The illustration is not a perfect one because, even if the forward end had wind of what had happened to the rear, it is possible that there would still be nothing better to do in the circumstances. But at least the unfortunate bee will serve to illustrate a failure of communications which interferes with the coordination of action. The interaction of the parts of an organism so as to conserve the identity of the whole we may call integration.[2]

The integration of Protestant institutions with the emergent picture of a new cultural mission calls for a new kind of Protestant press, in which readers would find a world that matches their own daily experience.

Even the aspects of controversy handled in the Protestant press are often made meaningless because of a careful and political balancing of factors. (The *Crusader's* portrait of a somewhat controversial Baptist leader, with its eagerness to dull the rugged edges, is a case in point.) Sometimes the press takes on

[2] Edwin L. Guthrie, *The Psychology of Human Conflict* (Boston: Beacon Press, 1962).

actually controversial matters of some importance, and handles
them well. Almost unanimously, the national Protestant periodicals acted responsibly in their counteraction of the threat from
the political radical right, which centered in attacks on churches
around 1961. The general record of the Protestant press on controversial racial issues is, we have reason to believe, considerably
ahead of the thinking of many denominational leaders, and certainly of much grass-roots (to use their favorite term) sentiment.
None of these examples should be minimized.

Most controversy on the pages of the Protestant press, however, is devoted to matters of less consequence. Of controversy
there is plenty. Let an editor portray Christ in modern art, and
his letters columns will be full of angry comment. If he wishes to
stir up controversy, let him say something critical of a Gospel
hymn, or take a decisive stand on clerical dress or the ceremonies
of worship. These sartorial and stage-directorial details have their
place. Liturgical finesse and esthetic appropriateness are not
small matters in the life of the church. People derive much of
their security from the changelessness of attachment to past
forms, and hate to have them jostled. But in a world of dramatic
social and cultural change, is it *really* important to debate
whether ministers should wear collars backwards or forwards?
This kind of pseudo controversy does, it is true, stir readers'
interests, but has little to do—whatever the outcome—with serious Christian goals. It provides a field in which the amateur, best
of all, can show his expertise. Everyone can know better than an
architect that "a church should look like a church," and everyone
can know that a Roman collar is Roman. But stimulating such
pseudo controversies further contributes to the cultural irrelevance which haunts the Protestant press from the outset.

The Protestant press is at its best when it works to understand
the secular culture, the ecumenical church, the need for dialogue;
when it is aware of its occasional secular readers, or conscious of
wanting to stimulate a general audience beyond the borders of
its own clientele.

These lengthy analyses of several magazines were designed to set the stage for a discussion of the real problem of the Protestant press. Such a discussion would serve the underlying purpose of this chapter: not to hand out awards or criticisms of specific products, but to question the context of the Protestant press. The basic problem of the mentality of the Protestant publisher, we have contended, is this: he seeks to define culture in Protestant terms, and to regret or denounce the emergent cultures which supplant Protestant forms. He defines his function precisely: he is to minister to a segment of the general public, that segment which supports the institution to which his periodical is attached. This audience is to be encouraged through his pages not only to support the institutional goals, but to interpret the world in the light of the importance attached to its effects and phenomena by the institution. The net result is a world of partial illusion in which inaccurate status-designations are assigned. He contributes to the split-level existence of his clientele. Despite the general excellence of his product technically, those who do not adhere to his institution can dismiss his publication out of hand, and many within it will hardly regard it seriously.

THE PROTESTANT PRESS
IN A PLURALISTIC SOCIETY

The basic fact of religious life in a modern free society is pluralism: "any number can play." The basic fact of American religious life, given its peculiar history, is denominationalism: "a great number are playing." In his mind every Protestant knows this. In his heart it has not taken sway, if we judge either from his conventional way of working day by day, or from the front he puts up to cultivate a self-image and a sense of purpose.

Every editor is aware that he lives in an age in which the communications revolution has occurred; he cannot go back ideologically to a primitive society, and in a practical sense, he is working every day within a technical society in which the media play a significant role. He comes to know that this revolution not only provides him with new technical means for reporting and propagating his witness; it also complicates the milieu. This understanding demands a radical reappraisal of all his claims. Superficial adaptation of terms and interests—"Baptists in the space age"—will not suffice. He, his institution, his doctrinal pattern cannot be taken for granted. Some may think, "if you leave things alone, you leave them as they are. But you do not. If you leave a thing alone you leave it to a torrent of change" (Chesterton). For the most, however, the editor is a victim of a first reaction to the communications revolution.

When the new technical breakthroughs in printing, postage, and broadcasting appeared against the assumed background of a Protestant culture, the publisher could say: I have the Gospel, the word to witness. I am now provided with a technique which helps me reach more people, a medium to do it. Therefore, I am provided with a larger audience, more open to these claims. But the second generation knows things have not worked out that way. It is more aware of the prior conceptions a public brings to the media; it knows about audience resistance and the defenses men present against propaganda. The religious publisher, insofar as his task is specifically Christian, suffers a further complication. His Gospel is, in some sense or other, seen to be *versus* the world. Were it wholly compatible with general market expectations, it would have been unnecessary. Jesus Christ, the Church, the evangelical witness, and the Protestant press which propagates that witness and reports on its forms—these are necessary to counter many expectations, to correct and even violate preconceptions and opinions. The Protestant press, however, against the presumed background of a Protestant culture, could afford to be less aware of this problem than it must be today against the background of a pluralist culture.

The Protestant press at the time of its birth had a right to see itself in the strictly defined terms of institutional function which many of its editors still hold. In previous centuries the immediate environment formed the "whole world." A Congregationalist magazine could enter a home and substantiate what a Congregationalist preacher would say to a Congregationalist community.

The assumptions of communicator and receiver were shared and were uncluttered by competing signals. The truth of the world picture and the particular witness were untested by exposure to Catholic, Jewish, secular media; to the orthodox voice in the World Council of Churches, the Lutheran family down the block, the ideology of the American Legion or the Kiwanis club. The essence of life after the technical revolution, in a crowded, mobile, interactive world is just that: interactive.

Today the recipient of a particular magazine is surrounded by signals which minimize the importance of its particularity. Now there are many forms of exposure and openness. Not that the new society is completely open. Men still need personal forms of resistance to the constant bombardments of the media; they insulate themselves and react against confusing signals by participation in socially integrating groups and sub-units of society. There are barriers, buffers, corridors, cuticles, layers, curtains which render particular messages muffled or diffuse. These corridors complicate communication in the religious press of today, just as they add to the efficacy of those communicating to specific subgroups. The communicator may minister well to *a* public or a segment of the public, but unless he reckons with *the* public he can face frustration and even the tyranny of a misunderstood and unchallenged public opinion.

In this argument, American society has taken on a peculiar form of pluralism. It is an open society that is not wholly open; it is an exposed society that is not really exposed. Religious institutions are in close, but not vital, contact with each other. The term *verzuiling*, employed by Dutch sociologists (J. A. A. Van Doorn and I. Schöffer among others), has come to characterize this mode of existence. *Verzuiling* refers to the columnization of life, the intersectioning of existence, the insulation pattern within an erosive society. While much of his thesis is extraneous to our current study, Will Herberg's contention that America has developed not a melting-pot culture, but at least a threefold, segmented ("Protestant-Catholic-Jew") culture, refers to a surprising, an unanticipated mode of pluralistic existence. Eugene

J. Lipman and Albert Vorspan, in *A Tale of Ten Cities; The Triple Ghetto in American Religious Life* (New York: Union of American Hebrew Congregations, 1962), underscore his findings. The most profound study of this type is Gerhard Lenski's *The Religious Factor* (New York: Doubleday/Anchor Books, 1962).

Sociologist Lenski made a study of the peculiar but pervasive influence religious groupings had on the economic, social, and political attitudes of white and Negro Protestants, Jews and Catholics in America by studying metropolitan Detroit. His conclusion pointed to a section of his last chapter entitled "Drift Toward Compartmentalization?" (pp. 326 ff.)

> Communalism along socioreligious group lines seems to have been gaining in strength in recent years, and promises to continue to gain in the foreseeable future.
>
> The findings of this study force us to consider the possibility that American society is moving (though admittedly slowly) towards a "compartmentalized society" of the type found in contemporary Holland and Lebanon, to cite but two of the more prominent examples. In these societies virtually all the major institutional systems are obliged to take account of socioreligious distinctions. Hence, political parties, families, sports teams, and even business establishments are generally identified with one or another of the major groups. . . . Society is organized like a series of parallel columns (*verzuiling*) or pillars.
>
> It may well be that compartmentalization along socioreligious group lines is the best we can hope for in a society which is religiously divided as ours is, if at the same time we are to preserve the values linked with the various subgroups. However, if given the group loyalties of Americans, compartmentalization is the best arrangement we can achieve, it would seem desirable that this alternative be chosen *after rational exploration and consideration of the alternatives.* Currently we seem merely to be drifting into a type of social arrangement

which Americans of all faiths might well reject if they became fully aware of all it entails.

This problem should be of special concern to religious leaders. Our current drift toward a "compartmentalized society" could easily produce a situation where individuals developed a heightened sense of religious group loyalty combined with a minimal sense of responsibility for those outside their own group. In a more compartmentalized society there is good reason to fear a weakening of the ethical and spiritual elements in religion and a heightening of the ever-dangerous political elements. Such a development would be a serious departure from the basic ideals of all the major faiths in America, sharing as they do in the Biblical tradition. Hence, on both religious and political grounds, Americans might do well to study, more critically than they yet have, the arguments advanced by advocates of pluralistic society.

We are indebted to Professor Lenski for posing, better than anyone else has done, the ideological and strategic question that confronts religious groups, and which should be applied to the situation of denominational journalism.

Much can be said in favor of *verzuiling,* the pillared, columned, curtained, and corridored existence in a bewildering society. Some element of it is absolutely necessary for the nurture of the child as he develops his view of the universe. Some remains necessary if particular faiths wish to be faithful to the varying generating centers of their faith, hope, and love. But it must seriously be asked whether there are not limits to its fruitfulness. Where, for example, does the Christian ask: When do I begin to use my vision of the City of God for the good of the City of Man?

Most of the forces in American religion in its institutional form minister to the compartmentalization of life, partly in reaction to the corrosive elements of the general religion, the consensus-faith, the sacred notions which pervade the public at the expense of religious faithfulness. This is healthy, so far as it goes and must go. The sermon, the church school, the ethos of the religious community, association, or subgroup—all of these quite naturally will be designed to provide identity and encourage faithfulness and loyalty. Should there not be some institutional instrument, however, which *counters* these natural forces and calls people to mission and service? Should not some agency exist to lead people, disciplined by private existence, into the public sphere? I would answer emphatically: The press is designed for that and suited for that. Here it fails its mission in Protestantism, if the foregoing critique is accurate.

The Protestant press, in the main, has committed itself to ministering to the compartmentalization and columnization of life in a free society. Unable to cope with pluralism and secularity as arenas for witness, taking refuge in the mythology of a past Protestant culture, for the most part it withdraws from the public arena. The City of Man exists as a missionary field from which some people should be plucked into the specific institutions. It exists as a foil, bogey, or contrast to help develop loyalties of those within the fold. But the press largely engages in building morale, nurturing group loyalty, and ministering to what Americans already instinctively engage in, at the expense of understanding a revolutionary world and participating in its dynamisms in the name of the Lordship of Jesus Christ.

An illustration offensive to Protestants might set the trend into bold outline. The standard criticism by Protestants, of Roman Catholic education in parochial schools, is this: How will children learn to participate in the larger free society? Where will they learn the elements that shape the democratic life, the aspects of consensus which cause a society to jell; whence will come the glue that holds together the common good, the lubrication for its processes? The Protestant (at least until Supreme Court decisions began to clarify this) saw the public school in the nineteenth century as his established church, and in the twentieth century as the established church of the generalized American religion. All his investments in a meaningful pluralism seem to be extended to the public school, and his criticisms fall on Catholic parochialism.

If we study the religious press, however, a certain suspicion grows. *Except* for the public-school–parochial-school matter, almost all energies of Protestantism as it is revealed in its press are devoted to the compartmentalized, corridored life. Take, as an instance, the cradle-to-grave, every-aspect-of-life nurture which a large denomination such as Methodism undertakes in its press. Most Methodists would criticize Catholics for developing a parasociety or a pseudo society alongside or within the whole or the real national community: parochial elementary schools, high schools, universities and colleges, insurance groups, sodalities, veterans' organizations, action groups of a political character, fraternal organizations, and so on. When does the Catholic participate in the free society on its own terms, understanding and serving it? The question, in Lenski's context, is disturbing and should be faced.

Can the Methodist (or a member of any other Protestant group) face it? His minister may boast that his church "has the lights lit every night," for church athletic leagues, men's and women's groups, benevolent societies, and so forth. For the most part, Christian laymanship is measured by the degree and quality of churchly life on church premises. This is understandable and in many ways justifiable. But to counteract this, one might look at the mass media, the interactive and nationally oriented forces such as the press. The Methodist Church has a parallel, a competitor for every kind of secular organ. *Together* competes for general interest with the mass magazines in family-life affairs. The *Christian Advocate* equips and informs Methodist ministers in their ministry. *Motive* is for the university student. *The Upper Room* provides for the devotional life. *The Methodist Layman* and *The Methodist Woman* solicit the energies of the genders. *Mature Years* points to lifelong concerns to shelter the Christian. *Religion in Life* is a scholarly journal, certainly one of the best. *World Outlook* summons missionary concerns of the denomination. The title of *The Christian Home* reveals its interest. *Concern* deals with Methodist social issues. A host of regional magazines, church school guides, and educational materials completes the picture. There is no place to hide.

Methodism is not to be particularly faulted for this compulsion to solicit the energies and minister to the needs of all sorts and conditions of men. All complex organizations tend to do this, and all Protestant denominations do. Does this not set upon the press, however, a special mission to nudge clienteles out of organizational concerns and into the culture and society where the energies, nurtured in the "columns" of church life, can be translated into action?

Unless this nudging happens, one must observe that there is only a quantitative, not a qualitative, difference between Protestant and Catholic attempts at parochialization and compartmentalization. It suggests only that the Protestant criticizes the Catholic for being a bit more inclusive, a bit more energetic than he himself is, by rounding out the circle of a self-important world in his establishment of parochial schools.

Since the public media and mass-circulation magazines minister so effectively to the consensus and cultivate the sacred notions in a society, at the expense of the Christian faith, the Protestant press is called upon to witness to that faith. This witness is undercut by the constant institutional appeal and the call for organizational loyalty. Competitiveness, self-seeking, the summoning of energies for minor goals, all detract from the more profound religious purposes of the press. Not that the press is a good instrument for conversion; it must content itself in the main with reinforcement, with preparing the ground for change of attitude, or for following through on personal mission. But these important indirect and secondary tasks cannot be undertaken by an "invisible" press or an organizationally self-oriented one. The press, equipped to relate people to culture and society, concerns itself with doing what local churches do better: relating themselves to themselves.

To pursue this question, we must ask: What would happen were the Protestant press to disappear tomorrow? There would have to be more tracts, more promotional material, more pro-grammatic folders from the headquarters of denominations and bureaus, since the Protestant press is extensively used to propa-gandize national organizational efforts. The directly functional aspects of the press would have to be supplanted by other means. But the non-Protestant public, hardly noticing the disappearance, would be served no less well by the Protestant community. The interpretation of life which the Protestant would now garner from secular media would more likely be somewhat more realistic, (though we are hesitant to confer too many congratulations on the realism of the secular press!). People's notions of reality and ways of conferring status on people and projects would per-haps be thrown into better adjustment. Ecclesiastical programs would bog down and loyalties or identities would become some-what more diffuse.

When we speak in these terms we try to remember the built-in limits of the media. Publishers are not gods, we remind our-selves. They cannot do everything. The secular press is not really a model. Every organ of opinion, every agent of particu-larity will have limits and boundaries, and must learn to live with them. If the Protestant press takes on a greater interest in the cultural and social involvement of people, and a greater interest in their theological (as opposed to organizational) understand-ing, it will be trading one set of limitations for another. But the new limitations will be more consistent with the inherent limita-tions of Christian witness—a choice Protestants are not supposed to be afraid to undertake.

Conversely, if the Protestant press does not disappear (and it shows no sign of intending to), what will be the future, if present trends continue? The press will continue to reproduce itself in an increased number of periodicals, in direct proportion to the in-creased number of units or projects Protestant groups assemble or undertake. If the Protestant press is directed to denomina-tional goals, to areas of specialization, and to avenues of direct functionality and purposiveness, the press will proliferate its products as the erosive forces around the churches multiply and the projects within grow more complex. The net result will be an ever-increasing contribution to the compartmentalization (*verzuiling*) of public life by the one agency in Protestantism which would be best able to counteract the tendency.

With Lenski we may say such a contribution may be a legitimate one, and it may be the one denominations consciously wish to effect: that ascertaining what is important in life be determined by organizational affiliation, and what should consume energies be determined along the same lines. But if this is the choice of the organizations and their press, it should be made more consciously and consistently than it has been in the past, and with less criticism of other agencies, religious or not, which are doing the same thing but sometimes with greater efficiency. Protestant inefficiency results from its bad conscience, its schizoid position. In its professed intention and in its self-understanding, Protestant Christianity wants its people exposed to the world for the sake of mission and service; it wants them to risk the Gospel in the hearing and hands of men; it is professedly ecumenical. These impulses are denied in the press when the whole thrust is toward organizational self-enhancement and protectionism.

THE HISTORICAL
PERSPECTIVE

Was it always thus? The Protestant press is not something new; it has been on the scene through much of the modern period. Are there clues from the history and experience of Protestantism that will explain the current American ambiguity?

The original impulse to place so much faith in the press lies deep in the origins and genius of Protestantism. Recall that the original Protestant revolt was against a pattern of authority which, it was felt, did not permit free dissemination of "the Word." We should also keep in mind that the central Protestant idea concerns the Christian belief that God acts on man's behalf in Jesus Christ, in order to rescue him. Man, in his impotence, cannot justify himself by his own efforts to keep the law of God.

The law accuses and annihilates man. The Christian good news says that God does not abandon man in His wrath, but restores, forgives, and redeems man, sending him out into life with hope and in freedom.

The chief corollary to this view of love and freedom, however, was and remains the belief that the ongoing embodiment of Christ, the institutional Church, does not possess the authority to restrict man in his access to the divine grace. No church laws, no ecclesiastical structures, no churchly traditions should carry the independent power to withhold from man these freedoms or access to the information and revelation by which his destiny is determined. The contrast to these two views was the medieval Catholic view of grace mediated through a particularly consolidated authority in the church, and a sacramental-hierarchical arrangement which limited man's access and freedom in relation to "the Word."

Modern Catholicism, of course, does not fit all the details of the foil against which the Reformation occurred. "Freedom of access" and openness to at least some degree of self-determination are fruits of the modern world, produced not only by Protestantism but also by a reforming Catholicism, the Enlightenment, and a practical situation in free societies. But the original impulse colors the later life of a group, and in Protestant mythology "the open Bible" and "the right of private judgment" still play a large, if distorted, role. Even if de-mythologized and corrected by changing historical emphases, Protestantism unanimously sees its impulse as one that is to be constantly criticized, corrected, and enhanced by dialogue with "the Word" and in words.

When words are misused, bound, restricted, cluttered, the Protestant vision and witness suffer. When the channels through which words come are misused, bound, restricted, or cluttered, the access to "the Word" is in danger. The press, because of its regularity, its competitive character, and its relation to the whole modern struggle for freedom, has symbolically and actually presented itself as an admirable instrument to Protestants.

The preached word is related to the public word. The preached word is beamed to a selected, partial public: the gathered and responsive community. The public word is beamed at a general, whole public. The former ministers chiefly to faith; the latter, to culture. The former cannot permanently enjoy the luxury of existence without the health of the latter. If the faith is regarded as culturally insignificant or irrelevant, it will less likely be regarded as a vital option in the matter of an eternal destiny.

Just as the printed word figures large in Protestant theology and faith, so it must be reckoned with in the study of culture and society. Luther's general word about the humane culture certainly applies to a function of the press:

> I am persuaded that without knowledge of literature pure theology cannot at all endure, just as heretofore, when letters have declined and lain prostrate, theology, too, has wretchedly fallen and lain prostrate; nay, I see that there has never been a great revelation of the Word of God unless He has first prepared the way by the rise and prosperity of languages and letters, as though they were John the Baptists . . . Certainly it is my desire that there shall be as many poets and rhetoricians as possible, because I see that by these studies, as by no other means, people are wonderfully fitted for the grasping of sacred truth and for handling it skillfully and happily. . . . Therefore I beg of you that at my request (if that has any weight) you will urge your young people to be diligent in the study of poetry and rhetoric.[3]

If Luther was more concerned with the relation of Christ to humane culture, Calvin and the English reformers were equally determined that the world of social affairs and political decision should involve and be illumined by Christians. Each used the printed page to propagate these relations of faith to its setting. Luther's role is best known, though the other reformers should

[3] *Luther's Correspondence,* trans. and ed. Preserved Smith and Charles M. Jacobs (United Lutheran Publication House, 1918), Vol. II, 176 f.

not be assigned a secondary status in their interest in the printed and published word. Luther wanted monasteries converted to libraries or book houses. Four hundred and thirty editions of the Bible or parts of it appeared in his lifetime. His tracts and pamphlets, nearest analogies to modern periodicals, were quickly disseminated. We know, for instance, that four thousand copies of his address, "To the Christian Nobility," were sold in five days in 1520—a figure which still would inspire an author today.

But the period of Bible dissemination, book publication, pamphlet production was but a forerunner of the later era when printing methods became more efficient and modern transportation made postal systems possible. The press as we know it did not exist in the Reformation century. But a new time was being born, a new "enlightened," technical, secular age; it had come into being during the century of the Reformation, and it began to spell the end of some of the Reformation's views of its own sheltered cultural setting. The Protestant genius in the realm of books (Luther; Calvin, *Institutes;* Milton, *Pilgrim's Progress*) has never been matched by superiority in or understanding of the press. Periodical literature grew up more largely independently of Protestant auspices, and often in contradiction to Protestant emphases. To this day the functions of periodical literature in Protestantism have not been wholly thought out, and history does not provide too many models for study.

The modern press, the modern concept of journalism, was born in the age after Christendom had already begun to disintegrate. The British, French, and German Enlightenment, even more radically than the Reformation, had faith in "the right of private judgment" (witness the move from Luther to Lessing); and this individualistic emphasis, to which we owe much that is good in the modern world, for all its limitations, stressed man's need to know and to know now. Faith in the power of exposure to an idea in a liberated context, and concern that the idea be presented to a large number of people and in a short period of time, led to the establishment in the eighteenth century of many of the enduring and classic forms of periodical and newspaper publication. Insofar as Protestantism participated in that culture of northwestern Europe, it adapted to these changes, changes which belonged basically to certain secular assumptions about man.

In the massive and inclusive sense of the term, the Protestant press was born in the nineteenth century, and the date of its birth still determines it. The modern world and all its secular possibilities and threats existed; these were in no small measure shrouded from the vision of Christians. They were in an expansionist mood, often an imperialist one. They were doing instead of thinking, acting instead of relating. Most of what they did can be regarded positively, but they left a legacy of problems in understanding, and the press belongs to these.

Nineteenth-century America saw the press explode as an agent and as a product of separation of church and state and its corollaries: religious voluntaryism, associationalism, competition, denominationalism.[4] The proliferation of competitive groups led to the radical increase in the number of religious periodicals, most of them Protestant, because Catholicism was a negligible minority in the early part of the century, and Judaism was hardly represented. Henry Smith Stroupe, in his study of the South Atlantic states' religious press (1802-65), lists sixty-four Baptist periodicals in this region alone. Presbyterians were second, Methodists third, Disciples of Christ fourth, and at least ten other denominations were represented. The religious tone of the era can still be gathered from them. For the most part they were polemic and proselytizing in character, tending to downgrade other Christian denominations. Long battles over religious viewpoints (that is, baptism of infants, immersion) were waged between them, and some news of the expansion of the churches is present. Through much of the period, southern attitudes toward the issues represented later in the Civil War were made clear.

Frank Luther Mott cites the period 1801-33 as the era of the "religious newspaper"—a weekly journal which mingled secular

[4] Still the best study of this complex of ideas is Sidney E. Mead's "Denominationalism: The Shape of Protestantism in America," in *Church History*, December, 1954.

news and religious miscellany, often more creatively than current denominational organs do. Mott declares that there were at least one hundred such newspapers around the country by the mid-thirties. Chief among them were the Congregational *Recorder* in Boston, the *Episcopal Recorder* in Philadelphia, the Methodist *Christian Advocate,* and the Presbyterian *Observer* in New York. Many of these later lost their vigor, died out, or were transformed into "cause" newspapers (e.g., for abolition) and changed their character. Even more remarkable, despite their brief existence, was the presence just before the Civil War of a number of religious dailies, some of which were related to the laymen's revivals around 1858.

In those days the exposed kind of Protestant press we are discussing here was in part not needed. While many freethinkers and community radicals gravitated to journalism and used it as their stronghold, most of the press reproduced the mores and thought patterns of the standard communities surrounding them. This means that, much like the early public schools, they were not really neutral in religion; their whole tone and religious emphasis looked Protestant. Much of the press was involved in the urban resentment against Catholic-Jewish immigration at mid-century, and it tended to raise issues in the name of Protestantism which today's secular dailies seldom would. In a Protestant culture, metropolitan newspapers, when in a religious mood, tend to take on some of the decorative externals of a surface Protestantism. But today's urban centers are not Protestant; their press reflects more of a pluralist pattern, placing the necessity of Protestant representation of interests and witness on the "invisible" church press.

Since the 1860s the religious press, according to Mott and others, has been almost exclusively denominational in orientation, with a few exceptions to be noted later. While the United States moved from denominationalism to pluralism in its self-understanding, the Protestant press still reflects much of the earlier phase. Today a general good will and ecumenical interest has overshadowed the old proselytizing and polemics. Of course, the press is still a convenient tool for the hate-monger. The *Christian Beacon* has served antiecumenical forces, and although *The Defender* has abandoned its earlier policy, *The Cross and The Flag* is still an instrument that helps perpetuate Protestant racism. But examples like these are hardly representative of Protestantism.

The ecumenical spirit and good will in the press can be traced to several sources. Most of the larger denominations are committed to the ecumenical movement, and in promoting it are doing their homework. Most of the editors are convinced that the unitive movement *is* the "great new fact of our era," and that if they really want to cover news, it will be Topic A. Most would agree that the Spirit of God has been signaling the churches' attention to the movement, and they support it for profoundly religious reasons. Still others recognize the growing level of contact between their clienteles; finally, some of the erosion of theological distinctiveness has worn off and the ecumenical movement seems to "come easy" except where it jeopardizes (or seems to) the autonomy of institutions.

Somehow the ecumenical interest is secondary, however. It is a mood, a reported-on event. The first energy still goes into individual denominations. The budgetary outlays of the various churches reveal this interest. Thus the ecumenical cause, which could rescue the Protestant press from its microcosmic preoccupation with the mirror, has not yet served as it might. What has often gone unnoticed is that meaningless particularism and unnecessary competition, as revealed in the attitudes of a denominational press, have actually tended to cancel out the seriousness of the theological quest. People grow weary on the cafeteria line of the faiths, determine that all are true and useful, and lapse into comfortable relativisms. Noisy exclusivism in the antiecumenical press contributes to this effect.

Denominationalism is absolutely determinative of the character of the Protestant press. Catholicism does not have this problem, nor does Judaism. Catholicism may have competition between clerical and lay papers, between diocesan and religious papers, between and within the orders. But a theological oneness relieves Catholicism of much of the burden Protestants have, except for the fact that the whole church is regarded as *a* denomination by the public. Judaism has many emphases and self-contradictory voices, but its press does represent a particular ethnic destiny that Protestantism, which "blends into the wallpaper," lacks. So Protestantism gets its distinctiveness from denominationalism, even in its trans-denominational press.

A book on the religious press cannot set out to solve the problem of denominationalism. The American pattern of separated church and state, voluntaryism, and independent churches has obvious strengths which no doubt must and would be preserved in any ecumenical fruition. Here it is necessary only to isolate the overpowering effect denominationalism has in determining the content and numbing the effect of the religious press. While most Christians would assert that the whole estate of Christ's church is their first concern, and that they should be the servants of others (Mark 10:43), the finances, time, energy, and preoccupation of the Protestant churches proceed inversely: first the self and the local church, then the denomination's programs, then possibly an interest in the ecumenical church and the world.

This self-centeredness leads to the kind of distortion that causes the mistrust with which denominational propaganda is regarded. Appearances must be kept up, the band wagon must roll, and the sponsoring church body is right and prevails. Anyone who reads the papers of several denominations can see how this self-importance of each group cancels out any seriousness with which their witness might be taken. Whoever would like to see this self-concern in its pure form would do well to canvass the papers of the Southern Baptist Convention!

The periodicals are not ordinarily audience-centered or witness-centered, but program-centered. When they are house organs for a denomination or agents for institutions, they are usually used to stimulate fund raising and carry out programs. Such propagandizing is of course the death of journalism, because of the distortion and misplacing of emphasis involved. It would seem more advisable that all programmatic material be divorced from the press, and the mailing lists be turned over to the propagandizing agencies—thus some sense of reality could be stimulated in the readers' minds. Denominational programs certainly are necessary. But if it is feared that independent mailings designed to stimulate them will be unread by constituents, so will programmatic materials inserted between articles of general interest in periodicals.

THE CHALLENGE
TODAY

If periodicals are not audience-centered or content-centered but programmatic, or related functionally to the institutional purposes of the moment, how do they hold interest? The "letters to the editor" columns of all magazines are notoriously unreliable guides to reader interest. Readers have a certain set of topics concerning which they will write whenever a reference occurs: fluoridation, antivivisection, anticommunism, the length of a stole, the choice of a hymn—each of these subjects stirs a private circle of interest. Meanwhile the more balanced reader is less inclined to take time to write letters.

Empirical studies and audience surveys are rather haphazard. Polls of readers on a voluntary return-card basis are no more accurate than letters-to-the-editor columns. A journalism school would do well to stimulate a more scientific scrutiny of what is read. Editors of the religious periodicals have considerable faith that their magazines are read; publishers and promoters, less certain of this, insist on "blanket subscriptions" and heavily subsidized transmission of information, in the hope that some percentage at least will be read.

If my observation is correct, the news holds greatest interest; feature articles are another area of superiority. Traditionally most of the periodicals feature some devotional material which is for the most part forgettable. In any generation only a few people are given the gift of producing devotional material of a superior nature; most of what appears looks like what I call "Sunday church bulletin style." The editor knows it is customary to fill a certain white space with piety, and he types out something or other on the theme of the month. That God may sometimes be better served by less chatter about God, and less moralizing, is a lesson that comes hard to those who are responsible for evangelical editing.

The non-Protestant who casually dismisses the Protestant press might be amazed at the quality of news and feature writing in many of the periodicals. The general excellence in this field is what causes such regret over the programmatic distortion forced on many an editor. Editorial sophistication is not just the property of the few. Were the reader given more guidance in sorting out the really important news from the routine coverage granted all ground-breakings, retirements, and local ceremonies, the Protestant press would deserve a wider reading.

Four samples will illustrate, all taken from magazines dated during September, 1962. The *United Church Herald* pictures Martin Luther King on the cover and features a long article on "Christian Direct Action" on the Albany, Georgia, racial front. It is hard to picture a mass-circulation secular magazine being so frontal in its coverage. An editorial reinforces the article. A feature on sacred music on records by William Robert Miller is an out-and-out rejection of Victorian standards of church music, and a discriminating affirmation of recent experiment. The third feature is a portrait of Hubert Humphrey, "A Christian Conscience in Politics." The fact that he belongs to the United Church of Christ is not touted compulsively; the stress is on conscience issues. Still another feature is truly esoteric, a report on a spiritualist encounter; it discusses ESP and related offbeat experiments and may be of doubtful value. Yet the "Spiritual Frontiers Fellowship" has raised some questions in the Protestant churches; this kind of "personal testimony" will add to the empirical data behind the discussion.

The *Herald*'s center spread is devoted to the forms of commitment which various ideologies and national interests assume.

Luther A. Weigle reviews a collection of Bible translations with authority and grace. One or two articles depict denominational colleges, programs, ministries, and ecumenical conventions. Not until page twenty-four does one encounter the specific denominational news; here non-U.C.C. members may find their interest dissipating. However, the editors have chosen several specific instances for parabolic treatment and given excellent brief captions to clear photographs. News of the world-wide Church is given equal space! Only the last two pages list the "official business" of pastoral changes.

Since the *United Church Herald* represents the merger between Congregationalist churches and the Evangelical and Reformed church, one should take cheer from this thoroughly professional magazine. I would without diffidence give it to anyone—Protestant, Catholic, Jew, agnostic—for a portrait of the kind of Protestant witness I would like to see prevail. The new magazine met with considerable resistance, some of it highly vocal from midwestern E. and R. churchmen who complained that the "city slickers" of New York had urbanized their organ beyond recognition and made it too "ecumenical." Too much of the folksy chit-chat had disappeared. Actually the *Herald* represents an at-homeness in the post-Protestant culture which others will have to seek.

If the *Herald* symbolizes the better trend which the ecumenical movement can bring to publishing by its necessary de-emphasis of the smaller denominations' private tribal rites, *The Lutheran* represents a continuing tradition of urbanism in its news and features. *The Lutheran* receives some of its freedom from its charter: covering and satisfying the needs of the large number of synods (each somewhat autonomous) that form the Lutheran Church in America. This has pushed the merely regional saturation-coverage news to the back of the magazine. Still, there is too much to give the magazine the real character which the first half promises. Page upon page of lists of commissions, maps, reorganization items of a purely routine character mar the September 19, 1962 (typical) issue. Reports from numbers of the synods give equal attention to the important and the trivial. The remainder of the magazine, while oriented more to Lutherans than to others, gives fair coverage of the Christian world. Only one of sixteen "spot" news items deals with the sponsoring denomination directly, but several others focus on world Lutheranism. The book reviews are of a high quality. Perhaps there is too much catering to "personal problems." The pat answers that must be dispensed in such short space violate most canons of counseling and probably appeal more to the "true confessions" taste than to the person who really has a problem.

Coverage of Washington and the editor's own page are stimulating every week. The features are related somewhat more to churchmanship than they were in the *Herald;* in most features, however, the world which church members meet when they step off the ecclesiastical premises is dealt with quite effectively.

The Episcopalian is an unashamedly Anglo-centered magazine with a "slick" face and format. Yet it has begun to serve as a model for the way it transcends some of these limitations and seeks to use denominational resources for the sake of others. Many of the impulses detected in the *Crusader* reappear here, though greater space in the magazine gives the opportunity for setting the accident of Anglican membership into context. Articles discuss the change in Ozark religion; the life of Henry Knox Sherrill, bishop and ecumenical leader; the Supreme Court's decision on school prayer—a really novel treatment; the Episcopalian who is Police Commissioner in Philadelphia; the genesis and metamorphosis of Christmas cards; the laity; the history of Anglicanism; a lay retreat. Since the Episcopal Church has been well located near many of the crossroads of recent events, the magazine looks less denominationally centered than it is. However, the non-Episcopalian who is looking for the Protestant press would weary sooner with it than he might with the *Herald* or even with *The Lutheran.*

More successful in orienting readers for life in the ecumenical era and in the world of decision has been *Presbyterian Life.* I know that it is casually dismissed among the middle-class "slicks" by the elite of journalist circles, but this is done more on the basis of stereotypical rejection than after scrutiny of actual content. Features in the September 1, 1962, issue include a popular discussion of "phoniness"; a portrait of an accomplished churchwoman; a report on new forms of summer camping; extensive coverage of the Supreme Court decision (which was handled more responsibly in press than in pulpit across the nation); and an article on the Peace Corps. The extensive and controversial General Assembly report on church and state was printed in full. News coverage of world and church is less provincial than in *The Episcopalian. Presbyterian Life* regularly includes features whose humor is more apt than most which appears in the Protestant press.

One may generalize: the more a denomination has been involved in mergers or in satisfying heterogeneous and urban clienteles, the more likely it will determine importance from this range of the spectrum:

1) the world around the church;
2) the whole church;
3) our denomination in the world and church;
4) our denomination acting independently.

The more a denomination has stood apart from merger (however "ecumenical" it may be in other respects), and the more it has been called upon to satisfy a provincial or homogeneous or rural clientele, then the more likely it is to reverse the order of importance. The trend seems to favor the larger perspectives; if the transition can be made without a concessionist catering to all interests, the future of the Protestant press looks more hopeful.

For the most part, editors do not deceive themselves into thinking that they are competing on even terms with the secular newspapers and mass magazines. More likely they seek to redress balances, to search out the religious dimension overlooked in the secular press, or to berate secularism. Sometimes their orientation calls for complaint concerning coverage in the secular press of urban emphases. This sulking has tended to diminish as Protestant editors have become more aware of the way publishing decisions are made. As recently as a decade ago, in the "first book . . . definitely focused on Christian journalism," Benjamin P. Browne could call for Christian writers to help Protestantism receive equal time: "A cold war is on," he wrote, " between Christian ideas and ideals and the utterly pagan propaganda and secular environment of our times. . . . We are plagued with unfair journalism. When Cardinal Spellman calls Bishop Oxnam a 'bigot,' the charge is printed on the front page of a New York newspaper. When Bishop Oxnam replies, it is hidden on an inside back page. Something about scandal among the clergy gets tremendous coverage. But to get favorable publicity for the Protestant clergy on the front page of a great metropolitan daily is almost as difficult as reaching the peak of Mount Everest."[5]

This kind of defensiveness toward the role of religion in the secular press may persist but is less frequently dealt with today in the Protestant press. Although aware of the causes which lead to the kind of unfairness of which Browne spoke, editors of Protestant magazines are less self-conscious, have more of a sense of business as usual, and sulk less about Catholicism.

Most of today's criticism of secularism mislocates the origins of secularism; fails to see the positive potentials in secularity; fails to see the ways in which the church's standards of succcess and avoidance of theological issues play into the hands of secularism. Unfortunately, the view of the secular world is distorted by the fact that, in all but a few journals, the only elements in the larger world which are dealt with are those that can be used as foils or exploited for gains. When a Presbyterian magazine spends all its energy showing that John Glenn is a Presbyterian (even an atheist can orbit, as Russia has shown!) instead of seeking to understand the meaning of the space age for the

[5] "Training Writers with a Christian Purpose," in *Christian Journalism for Today* (Philadelphia: Judson Press, 1952), pp. 13 ff.

church, it heightens the sense of exploitation and unreality. Meanwhile the chatter, gossip, and suburban-news chit-chat which displace discussion of a revolutionary world separate readers from significance.

The contributors to this volume have been asked to draw up a balance sheet of achievement and liability. What does the Protestant press do well; what does it do badly? Much of this has already been commented upon, but such a summary may clarify.

The Protestant press (except for several public instances) does well at building loyalty, ministering to enclaves, encouraging morale, producing articles of technical efficiency. Within the contexts of denominational self-obsession, the editors sometimes serve as correctives and at least make the most of a difficult situation. They seek to redress some imbalances which the more stridently promotional departments of church institutions effect in clienteles. They have attracted men whose professional competence is seldom secondary to that of men in similar posts in the secular press; most of them have a dedicated sense of vocation. Now and again (against the radical right, against the anti-Supreme Court ranters, on racial matters) they are the most responsible voice in the denominations. They set out to fill a specific function and fulfill that function well; they nurture the separate families of Christian churches without regard for eavesdroppers or public.

The Protestant press (except for several public instances) does badly at presenting major secular events and news of the ecumenically oriented church with real seriousness. It tends to confer the wrong status on persons and events in proportion to the nearness of these persons and events to denominational concerns. It encourages the ecological imprisonment of Protestants in suburban and middle-class settings. It is insular more than it needs to be in its work down the corridors between the pillars of a compartmentalized society. It fails to help break down compartments or to lead Christians out into the arena. It is defensive about the situation of Protestantism and Christianity in the world. It is edgy in the presence of irony or humor; most humor in the Protestant press can best be characterized as mediocre and "cute."

What is crucial is how the editors see the saeculum, how they relate the present age to the Christian faith. When an editor (as in the *United Church Herald*) sees secularity not merely as enemy or foil but as a positive potential, he brings us closer to the moment when the Protestant press must be taken seriously. "Christian preaching from unexpected pulpits" is regularly reported in the *Herald, Presbyterian Life,* and a few other magazines in their coverage of drama, theater, art gallery. But most magazines are reluctant to carry their readers into this world and are more concerned to minister to existing "rural" attitudes toward the world of cultural expression.

The degrees of relation to authority vary widely. In general the more "liberal" denominations allow a greater freedom to the editors, but that generalization is subject to many exceptions, and a good number of conservative editors stride with exemplary freedom in their own contexts. The "house organs" quite naturally are mouthpieces for their institutions, though here too the more artful editors have learned the grace of creative foot-dragging and creative nudging. One would not expect a denomination to subsidize a journal that would run counter to its purposes; what is looked for here is the part the press can play in enlarging a denomination's purposes! If my observations and accounts of interviews are accurate, authoritarian censorship is seldom the problem in Protestant editing. Subtle pressures of organizationalism and unspoken guide lines or untested taboos are more frequently the agents which limit imagination. The ecumenical attitude does not necessarily free editors from subtle censorship. Often organs of interchurch agencies are not made more free by the heterogeneity of sponsors and clientele. They sometimes create bland products in order to pacify the many elements which make up an interdenominational agency. Censorship is not the basic problem of the Protestant press; nor is authoritarianism. More pervasive is a willing capitulation to the halfhearted, low-bore goals of denominational programmatic life.

When the editors use the freedom that is theirs by theological right as Protestants and by organizational charter in the more far-seeing institutions, will they then be free to serve their communities? I say, yes. They will be serving their communities better than they now are, better than the communities deserve, better than they may at first understand. The Biblical assumption behind this chapter is found in a concrete word in the Fourth Gospel:

> Truly, truly, I say to you, unless a grain of wheat falls into the earth and dies, it remains alone; but if it dies, it bears much fruit. (John 12:24)

Denominations, institutions, organizations of all sorts in the Christian context possess identities which remain valid if they exist for others, for God in Christ. Editors who would contend that my argument is "anti-institutional" will have misread it. What disturbs the non-Protestant or the reader of the organs of other institutions is the widespread preoccupation with the image, the goals, the nurture of the individual unit for its own sake. Occasional rhetorical flourishes to the contrary do not dispel the massive conclusion which any content analysis reveals. The sub-community is ministered to more than the community, the *Gesellschaft* more than the *Gemeinschaft,* the "natural" cell more than the theologically inclusive cell.

The Protestant witness derives its vision from the fact that "our commonwealth is in heaven" (Phil. 3:20); its source is in the fulfilled life. This gives the Christian the charter to move with responsibility and freedom in the midst of and for the sake of the earthly commonwealth. Protestantism contends for the life free of clericalism, hierarchical obsession, and ecclesiastical control, so that its vision of the eternal "city . . . whose builder and maker is God" (Hebrews 11:10) may motivate the servant of God in the temporal city.

When it seeks to shape such a life and such a mission, the

Protestant press will aid in the formation of the only kind of Christian whose life in the City of Man will be understood. Equipping the Lutheran to rejoice in Lutheran beauty queens, the Methodist to glory in the Methodist All-America team, or the Presbyterian to rally around Presbyterian astronauts suggests a compulsion to "belong" in the earthly society on superficial terms. It actually seeks to use the world for the sake of the church group; to exploit the possibilities the world offers; to prove what the world is not curious about in the first place.

Failure to draw the attention of the public press to the Protestant cause (as Benjamin Browne complained) was in part the result of the fact that Protestantism was not, for a time, "doing anything." The fund-raising campaigns, new buildings (if not architecturally distinguished), and smorgasbords of the evangelical churches did not deserve the public attention. Protestants no longer need complain about public disinterest: sit-ins, bus rides, inner-city missions, missions of service in the name of Jesus Christ and under evangelical church auspices have been splashed all over front pages. There are energy resources in the environment which Protestantism can legitimately use and minister to; when it does so, it does not have to ask for attention, and will not seek it.

Failure to understand the fact that congruity with the servant-hood of Jesus Christ best serves the world and attracts the concern of the world is behind much of the defensiveness of the Protestant press. Wailing over cultural change, regretting the fact that men do not bring all their hopes to the churches, conceiving of the churches as holding operations—all these attitudes relate to denominational introversion and thus are unnecessary. It is the press that can best show this and say it—if it cares to.

To illustrate: Protestant Christianity can stand at the side of the other agents in a free society, ministering with its views of freedom and separation of aspects of church and state. Some editors have been doing this (Presbyterian leaders are prime examples). But the general public does not see this, because the history of Protestant publishing has found its press on the side

of self-defensiveness over against Catholic intrusions in the field
of church-state relations. I am sure that the growing understanding of pluralist possibilities will free more and more segments of
the Protestant press from such misplaced militancy.

Again: Protestantism, in its understanding of social change
and its witness—in changed circumstances—to humane concerns
(in a world of hunger) and to stewardship of the world's resources, has important and positive words to say on the subject
of limiting population growth. Until the recent past this was dis-
regarded by the public, which saw chiefly an opposition to Catholic birth control doctrines in the Protestant stance.

In the world of ideologies, as a committed evangelical Christian I believe Protestantism has much to say to the concrete
aspirations of man, aspirations which are now so tragically
misplaced in the Communist world. So much of Protestantism's
public face has been concerned with catering to the insulated,
middle-class location of American nationalist churches that it has
been limited in confronting the basic question. More recently,
editors of Protestant journals courageously withstood the popular
forces which, in the name of nationalist selfishness, forbade even
recognition of the hungers and needs of underdeveloped areas at
home and abroad. In 1961, many editors risked their situations in
order to speak a free and bold word, sometimes against their
richest supporters. This kind of courage will serve to make the
Protestant press visible.

Still another illustration: The Protestant press was regarded
traditionally as a defender of Puritan "blue" laws in the matter
of pornography, Sunday closing, and the nation's mores. The
emerging generation of editors, by no means libertarian in outlook, has been increasingly willing to understand the motivations
of modern literary artists and has often sided against police
censorship—in doing so, even going against its own taste. A
good number of Protestant editors who found Henry Miller's
work offensive, nevertheless contended against suppression of
his writing. This kind of new concern which transcends personal

prejudices will free the Protestant press to say a positive word on the future of the nation's standards.

If in the nineteenth century the Protestant press was often overtly anti-Semitic, this has changed in recent times. Increasingly, anti-Semitism has been pointed out as the basic sin in relation to Our Lord's humanity; across the denominational lines the press has gone out of its way to beat back anti-Semitic elements in fringe Protestantism. As this happens, since some Jewish participation in a free society will limit the uniquely Protestant or Christian understanding of culture, the Protestant press will be seen to be a servant and not a self-seeker.

In public affairs, there is no question but that realization of the implications of pluralism has affected Protestant editors more than it has their clienteles. The Protestant press is less anti-Catholic, less anti-Jewish, less anti-social-change than the constituency of the denominations, as will be evident to anyone who observes a layman's group denouncing an editorial board for its view of a mission to the nation and the world. This is not to say that the denominational or independent magazines are very often "liberal" in politics; certainly none of them are Marxist in orientation, as were some in the 1930s (e.g., *The Protestant*). But in the main-stream denominations, in those affiliated with the National Council of Churches, the press belongs to what Richard Rovere would call "The Establishment." It tends to support the United Nations more or less enthusiastically, and a slightly left-of-center foreign policy with only some reserve. If Peter Berger, Gibson Winter, Gerhard Lenski, and the other sociologists are correct, this is not so true of Protestant congregations across the board.

Most editors have learned the art of appeasing their clienteles and slightly nudging them forward in churchmanship. Denominational narcissism has kept them from realizing the full potential of doing the same in "worldsmanship." Controversial positions are ordinarily argued in a clientele-pleasing context. The World Order Study Commission of the National Council of Churches, which tiptoed toward supporting the admission of Red China into the United Nations, has been treated gingerly by most of the press, more often from prudential reasons than from a desire to understand the situation. Indulgence in pseudo controversy (liturgical affairs, size of budgets) has diverted attention from the press's task of raising basic questions.

Any denominational editor could rightly defend himself by asking, "Where are these models in the secular world?" Isn't this the day of homogenization, of pseudo events, of studied unreality in the world of advertising, of bland monopoly in the metropolitan press? I would answer: Exactly. The secular press today does not provide many models for emulation and inspiration. That is simply not the question addressed to the churches, which are to derive their norms from a point beyond the norms and standards of the existing community. The wastelands and barren stretches, the superficialities and the safe refuges of the secular press today should provide a greater charter for the church press if it is ready to take the risk.

THE INDEPENDENTS

Most of the concentration in this chapter has been on the institutionalized Protestant press. This may have been a surprising choice to the non-Protestant, to whom this press is virtually invisible. But it is safe to say that 95 per cent of subscriptions, advertising dollars, subsidies, and financial energies are invested in this portion of the press. What about the independents? A brief series of case studies may be introduced here to suggest some alternatives within Protestantism and to point, for all the minuteness of most of their subscription lists, to some clues for a more exposed evangelical press.

A first illustration is *Christianity and Crisis,* a slim, low-budget venture that has come out of the Niebuhrian circle at Union Theological Seminary. While its subscription list has only recently reached 10,000, the magazine has public influence greater than the denominational magazines with hundreds of thousands of subscribers. The influence proceeds in a twofold manner. The magazine influences the people who influence the culture through strategic location. In addition, secondary contact through the newsmaking it indulges in, as reported in the wire services and the news magazines, brings it to a larger public.

Christianity and Crisis represents, it is true, only one element in Protestantism. Urban, sophisticated, wise to the world of power, generally liberal in orientation, it would hardly be recognizable as a Protestant organ in many a faithful upper midwestern congregation. But by self-definition the magazine, under the editorship of Wayne Cowan, seeks to proceed from the community of Christian faithfulness into a real world where political, economic, and cultural decisions are made. It serves the whole church in seeking to show that the faith is not culturally trivial.

Christianity Today is in a somewhat more illusory relation to the world at large. Through mass gift subscriptions (wealthy laymen subsidize it to the extent of $225,000 a year), and through secondary contact via the news media, it has come in recent years to be regarded as the chief spokesman for what is styled "neo-evangelical" Christianity. Under the energetic editorship of Carl F. Henry, it has rallied great numbers of Protestant clergymen to its post-Fundamentalist Reformed conservative position. Because of its Biblicism and political conservatism, it has also enjoyed the strange bedfellowship of circles of Episcopalian and Lutheran churchmen to whom its theological position on revelation would seem heretical.

It differs from *Christianity and Crisis,* or the nondenominational *Christian Century,* in that it is a symbol, a rallying point, for an intra-Protestant political viewpoint, whereas the others seek to provide a forum in which questions of wider scope are asked. *Christianity Today* has served well to articulate the theological viewpoint of that element of the Protestant clergy which is resisting the ecumenical movement and the social involvement of the churches. The degree of rationalist individualism (which has been equated with the Christian Gospel) that is present in conservative Protestant clerical circles is recognized on its pages.

While its position is predictable because of its compliance with the social position of its sponsors, *Christianity Today* has through the years drawn closer to the interfaith dialogue. Originally it sounded like a press release from the Formosan embassy; this entrenched position is by no means so obvious today. Originally it opposed virtually every move the non-Catholic ecumenical councils made; today it is more ambivalent, though it cannot resist a suspicious sniff at most turns. Originally it was completely defensive about a Protestant culture; now it has taken more open positions on matters of church and state and the understanding of American culture. Without question, as the public expectation is in part extended toward the conservative spokesmen, *Christianity Today* will find itself more and more in the exposed position which this chapter has advocated as a possibility for Protestants.

The *Christian Herald*, edited by Daniel A. Poling, represents another public face of the Protestant press. It is less quoted in the news media than the other three journals under discussion at this point, but this results in part from its choice of subject matter and its market. By far the most successful independent (431,000), it represents a generally conservative theology, but one that is more diffuse and less articulate than *Christianity Today*'s. The best way to put it is: This is a Protestant version of the theology of the *Reader's Digest*. Suspicious of social change, world revolution, and "the welfare state" at home, it touts the virtues of "individualism." It is chiefly preoccupied with the private sphere—personal problems, child care, and family life. In the public domain it is ordinarily anti-Catholic and defensive about Protestantism's status. It is generally chauvinistic in outlook. Like *Together* and *This Day* in the denominations, it is rooted in the middle-class patterns of the American Protestant majority and is careful not to upset the pattern seriously. It is notable chiefly for its commercial success, a tribute to its modes of promotion and its understanding of the Protestant market's preconceptions. It verges on the public exposure of which we have spoken.

The Christian Century has had a unique history. Competing for a place in the public life of the nation at the side of *America* and *The Commonweal* among Catholics; *Christianity and Crisis* among Protestants; and *The Nation, The New Republic,* and *The National Review* in the secular field, it has been published weekly for half a century (with a negligible subsidy by individuals or institutions who are given no say in the policy), and has a circulation which reaches, at best, 40,000 subscribers. Without question, it is the most quoted and most public of the examples of the Protestant press. I should like to be sufficiently subjective to say that it incorporates at its best many of the virtues among the opinion journals that I should like to see evident in transformed ways among the mass-circulation magazines. I should also be sufficiently objective to say that its choice of status as an independent journal of opinion will limit it from becoming a mass organ, and it must leave to others the creative steps in that direction.

Some of what I have said to the general reader along the way will no doubt be lost on the Protestant editors of the non-independents, who will feel that my orientation is too much identified with *The Christian Century.* Actually there is no one on the present staff of the magazine who does not see problems in its past and present which limit it from taking on the larger burden of the Protestant mass-produced press. Therefore, because of its completely independent base and institutional freedom, I have been careful not to use it as the model for measuring the Protestant press.

This exclusion should not prohibit me from referring to those elements in the magazine's history which have poised it to serve Protestantism. It has really lived in three eras. Under Charles Clayton Morrison, its founder, in the early years of the century it belonged (as its title suggests) to the hopeful liberal school which saw for Protestantism a larger place under the economy of God on earth than a revolutionary world permitted it. Morrison had a genius for locating the magazine at those junctures and sore points in social life where it could participate in freedom. Under Paul Hutchinson it still spoke chiefly to Protestantism on "closed-circle" terms, but it was moved into a world where the odds against Protestantism were seen to be increased. *The New Ordeal of Christianity*, the title of a book by historian Hutchinson, reveals his realistic awareness of the milieu.

Under its third editor, Harold E. Fey, the magazine moved from the Protestant cultural setting into pluralism. Its representations of Catholicism are often regarded as limited by its earlier vision, though a radical change in its attitude toward the theological and personal sides of Catholicism has been apparent. Liberal in civil rights and racial matters, as well as in questions of censorship and free speech, it has begun more and more to speak to Protestantism and non-Protestantism with less interest in "closed-circle" appeal. It has tried, as a recent expression of a Catholic editor put it, to interpret pluralism to Protestantism, and Protestantism to pluralism. In ecumenical affairs it has moved from a simplistic solution to a theological concern somewhat along the lines of the Faith and Order emphasis. Politically it may appear to be more pragmatic, less doctrinaire, than was its public image two decades ago; this is a reflection of a change in options in American life, and a general disaffiliation from ideological causes. Theologically it serves more as a form than a rallying symbol, promoting a theological dialogue in the contexts of present-day ecumenical thought.

Devoted to the Protestant churches and the ecumenical movement, its freedom from institutional ties and its self-critical stance prevent it from attracting a sufficiently broad financial base to permit it all the experiment in which it should engage. Yet even its detractors agree that it would be hard to picture Protestantism without the forum or the arena it presents. *The Christian Century* will also have to walk in newness of life as it realizes all the implications of pluralist society. Keeping the faithful clientele it has developed in Protestantism for three generations, while moving toward the emergent theological and ecclesiastical generation, will require skill, and may involve some difficult choices.

Social questions of our time are not as clearly black-and-white as during the period when the Social Gospel of the magazine's past developed its public position. Today cultural decision is often just as important in determining what is man, and what is society. During the past decade the magazine has begun to amplify its cultural stance in editorials, articles, and features. While still reluctant to take on the really new elements in culture—"the theater of the absurd," abstract art, and some of the facets of urbanism—it has had some difficulty justifying these "secular" concerns to a part of its readership. How it resolves these ambiguities will make for an interesting future, in which I hope to take a part.

If *The Christian Century* has been the most public element in the Protestant press in the last half century (any bibliography of Protestant social thought will make this clear), it will not easily be able to continue to hold this position without more company in other genres. A *Christian Science Monitor*—that is, a daily paper in which Protestantism moves with finesse and freedom in a world where it must forgo many institutional preoccupations —we have seen to be out of the question at present.

Two other futures have more possibility. One would be a weekly newspaper, much like the German *Christ und Welt*, whose social interests are similar to *The Christian Century's* in the United States. But both positively and negatively, the German magazine is less interested in ecclesiastical life and more interested in culture on its own terms. Illustrated, in newspaper format, it could present a whole different range of Protestant concerns to a larger audience than *The Christian Century* now does, without overlapping on the *Century's* field. One hesitates to use *The National Observer* as a model. Whatever its limitations, its format and its market outlets suggest new directions for a Protestant venture.

Another alternative would be an independent mass-circulation magazine, to compete not with the Luce magazines (we are not dreaming) or with the women's magazines (as the *Christian Herald* aims to do), but directed to the increasingly literate market attracted to magazines like *The Atlantic, Harper's*, or *The Reporter*. In short, somewhere between *Christianity and Crisis* or *The Christian Century* and the mass market, it could be an "intermediate range" missile. The Roman Catholic *Jubilee* has incorporated some of these concerns, without yet finding exactly the needed formula.

Who should publish such a newspaper or magazine? One would imagine that a large publishing concern, one that has begun to discover the new kinds of book markets, would have the experience, the capital, the sense of venture needed. In light of the denominationally-oriented hold on funds with which Protestantism is beset today, it is hard to imagine church-based ventures "out into the world on its terms."

CONCLUSIONS

This speculation may seem to represent a dream world. But all through this chapter we have implied certain stances which could help the existing Protestant press develop new responsibility. Let us assume that the evangelical press is interested in keeping its existing strengths; what could occur to enhance its service?

1. Consolidation of periodicals. There are too many saying too little of consequence to too few. The *United Church Herald* is certainly worth more than the two magazines it supplants, as is *The Lutheran Standard.* Boards and bureaus of denominations could consolidate their energies into a less programmatic but more fruitful cluster of magazines.

2. More venture by Protestant churches, foundations, and individuals in the independent press. For all its independence and self-critical stance, by those virtues the press serves Protestantism in the larger public.

3. Redirection of energies. If every institutional editor envisioned a market outside his own denomination in every line he published, many of the current vices of the Protestant press would be removed by a simple habit of mind.

4. Consider dropping "saturation" news which trivializes the whole enterprise. Protestant editors could employ supplements, throw-aways, and newsletters to report on routine items. Most of these are designed to satisfy the interests of the people named in

them, or to provide ephemeral but necessary intelligence for leaders in the institution. Magazines would be freer to concentrate
on parables, to feature hard news of a more important type, to
focus on human interest (the picture of one man is human interest, of three hundred, a statistic.)

5. Employ fraternities such as the Associated Church Press,
which has done much to improve the quality and situation of
Protestant publishing, to new ends. Instead of spending so much
time discussing techniques and superficialities, at which the
Protestant press is already good, it could devote more energy to
"the thing" itself: what do we have to say, to what kind of person
in what kind of world?

6. Devote similar energies to creative experiments in religious
journalism, such as the Green Lake Writers' Conferences, and the
School of Religious Journalism at Syracuse University. These
devote themselves at present chiefly to the technical side,
whereas the ideological and cultural question is still slighted.

Protestantism best engages in mission and service where it
exposes itself to the world not as a triumphant institution in a
"business as usual" stance, but as a servant of the world in which
Jesus Christ is Lord. If the press does not jog the churches
to present this authentic public face, who will? The individual
Christian can, in his individual vocation. But he is often alone,
unministered to. The rest of the institutional complex has other
assignments, or can hardly be granted the vision to see this one.

The Protestant churches deserve a self-critical press; the national community would be better served by one. The vitalities
and technical competences of the editors, so visible to someone
inside the fraternity, do not often reveal themselves to the public.
The Protestant press becomes better and better at what it has
long been good at: ministering in the columnized, compartmentalized, corridored life of the churches. If it can move with
freedom to portray an evangelical style of life, the hiddenness of
the Christian faith could be exposed to public view. That is the
function of the Protestant press.

2 The Catholic Press:

THE WHY AND THE WHEREFORE

JOHN G. DEEDY, JR.

MAKE no mistake about it, the Catholic press in the United States is big business. Since 1808, when a printing press and a font of type were purchased in Baltimore and carted over the Appalachians to Detroit to print the first Catholic paper in the United States, the Catholic press has grown into something of a colossus. The *Catholic Press Directory 1962–63*, the official media reference guide of the Catholic Press Association, places the combined newspaper and magazine circulation of the Catholic press in the United States at a whopping 26,953,511. This figure represents the production of 130 newspapers and 371 magazines; it reflects the active commitment of all but a handful of dioceses and religious orders; it involves the talents and energies of tens of thousands of men and women, both in an official and unofficial capacity; it accounts for the flow of millions of dollars through the country's economy. As a dollars-and-cents proposition, the Catholic press is a substantial item.

But except for accidental fact, the Catholic press does not exist as an economic prop; the Catholic press exists to serve definite apostolic purposes, some of them selfish, some of them humanitarian, and all of them bound up with or complementary to the Church's evangelical and social missions. At different stages in history emphases have varied to meet the challenges posed, but throughout, the aspiration has been to function as a sort of modern Gospel, chronicling and promoting the activity of the Mystical Body of

Christ (the Church), as the four Gospels chronicled the activity of the physical Christ.

In the light of such an aim, the Catholic press's record over the years has been at best uneven. On occasion it has risen, almost literally, to great heights, but at other times it has become so cantankerously enmeshed in negative preoccupations and so absorbed in trivialities as to convey the impression, to borrow Jaroslav Pelikan's words, that there is "nothing more sectarian and less universal than the Roman Catholic Church."[1] One unhappy consequence is that the Catholic press in the United States has never achieved a status and influence commensurate with its circulation.

The story of Catholic journalism in America falls rather neatly into three chapters: the immigrant phase, during which the primary challenge was to guard the faith of Catholics and to defend the Church against calumnies; the post-immigration period, during which the Catholic press came tightly within the orbit of Church authority; and finally, the modern period of fermentation during which the Catholic press responded to the political, spiritual, and intellectual urgencies that followed World War II. The first chapter covers the nineteenth century and closes with the promulgation of Leo XIII's "Testem Benevolentiae," the encyclical which settled the Americanism controversy, but which also had the effect of dropping a blanket of silence over the Catholic press; the second carries roughly from 1900 through World War II; the third dates from the war and extends at least to the opening of Vatican Council II in the Fall of 1962. Since then there are indications that the "fresh winds" of the Council may have blown the Catholic press in America into a new and exciting fourth phase. Enthusiasts describe this as the "open window" phase, and such it very well might turn out to be. Certainly many windows of the Catholic press are open wider than any of them have been in decades, and news and opinion

---

[1] Jaroslav Pelikan at the 1962 convention of the Catholic Press Association, as reported by N.C.W.C. News Service, May 21, 1962.

which once would have been confined behind shutters now are exposed to air and the light of day. Whether this is a passing phenomenon or a condition that is to endure, it is too early to predict. A number of factors are involved, including the durability of the spirit of frankness and the anxiety to communicate, which Pope John XXIII brought to the Council. In any instance, the new freedoms are welcome, and they cause editors and readers alike to look to the days ahead hopefully and with fascination.

Nothing contributed more immediately to the emergence of a Catholic press in America than the fact that Catholics were strangers in a strange land, and unwelcome strangers at that, amidst a culture which was overwhelmingly Protestant and hostile to many values, religious and otherwise, that Catholics held dear. The initial problem was to conserve the faith of these people and to protect them and their Church against an ugly bias which had physical as well as political and social overtones. Indeed, such were the animosities against Catholics, it is not surprising that their press should have become infused with a vibrant polemical character, which became so pronounced that traces endured long after the necessity or justification had dissolved.

Catholics were no exception to the unwritten rules by which virtually every immigrant group settled in America. It took them a long time to recognize that they could not make of their new situation an extension of the homeland. Catholic publications played party to this folly by catering to the nostalgias, culture, and nationalism of the particular immigrant group served. The latter tendency was so strong in the Catholic press that there was frequently cause to wonder whether a given publication was first Catholic or first Irish, German, French, and so on.

Actually, there were no apologies or pretenses about the identification of the religious press in America with the culture and causes of the homeland an ocean away. Hence Bishop John England of Charleston cited in 1832 the objectives of ". . . the first

American Catholic newspaper properly so called":[2] "The writer would add that during upwards of ten years he and his associates have, at a very serious pecuniary loss, not to mention immense labour, published a weekly paper, *The United States Catholic Miscellany*,' in which *the cause of Ireland at home and Irishmen abroad*, and of the Catholic religion through the world, has been defended to the best of their ability."[3] (Italics added.)

Likewise, the Catholic publication which today claims to be the oldest in the United States, *The Pilot*, in Boston, was known in 1834-35 as *The Irish and Catholic Sentinel*. Though the Irish tag was aborted and the paper's name changed eventually and permanently to *The Pilot*, concern with things Irish was to endure for generations. In 1870, for instance, *The Pilot's* Irish dispositions were such that it assigned a "war correspondent" to cover the Fenian invasion of Canada from St. Albans, Vermont, and Malone, New York.[4]

That nationality groups could thrive as islands in nineteenth-century America is proved by the foreign-language Catholic press. Not only could a strong weekly press be built (the *Ohio Waisenfreund* once claimed the largest circulation of a Catholic weekly in the United States), but boast could be made of a healthy daily press. This press enjoyed enormous influence among ethnic groups, but the very element which guaranteed success—the native language—presaged its doom and at the same time the increased detachment of Catholics from the main stream of American life.

Looking back now, one of the curiosities of those years is the absence from the Catholic press of any strong notion of solidarity in faith or in patriotism. Catholic readers too often were first Irish or German or Slovak, then Catholic and, almost in afterthought, American. Except in isolated instances (notably *Brown-*

[2] John Tracy Ellis, *Documents of American Catholic History* (Milwaukee: The Bruce Publishing Co., 1956), p. 232.

[3] *The Catholic Encyclopedia*, Vol. XI, 692.

[4] James Jeffrey Roche, *John Boyle O'Reilly, His Life, Poems, and Speeches* (New York: Cassell Publishing Co., 1891), pp. 107 ff.

son's Quarterly Review) there was no appreciable effort to forge
a distinctly American image; the hyphenated Catholic had his
hyphenated Catholic press, absorbed in Old World causes and
attitudes that spilled over into competitions, jealousies, and
frictions in the New.

These nineteenth-century intramural Catholic controversies
were multiple, exciting, and riotous to such a point that at times
they assumed the proportion of public scandal. Bishops argued
with one another, priests took their independent positions, laity
battled for power; and the Catholic press, in the thick of the
melee, was no moderating influence. William L. Lucey, S.J., comments on the Catholic press's "carping criticism" of the hierarchy,[5] and Thomas L. McAvoy, C.S.C., speaks of "rough and
perhaps undignified" exchanges between Catholic editors.[6] It is
worth noting that there was no general or organized attempt to
suppress the Catholic press's right of involvement or of free
speech. The American bishops, in council at Baltimore and later
in meeting at Chicago, urged discretion on the editors, but there
was a tolerance in their cautions, and no formal intrusion.

The era of debate and recrimination declined with the publication of "Testem Benevolentiae," Leo XIII's apostolic letter of
January 22, 1899, to Cardinal Gibbons, which praised the spirit
and the progress of the Church in America, but which deplored
the "contentions which have arisen . . . to the no slight detriment
of peace." The letter was not addressed exclusively or even
specifically to the Catholic press but did help to breathe a new
character into it; there was a speedy metamorphosis and the
swashbuckling Catholic press of the nineteenth century entered
the twentieth subdued and reserved, if not completely docile.

During the nineteenth century the Catholic press may not always have served the Church judiciously; it may frequently have
responded defensively to challenges which were positive, but it

[5] In *An Introduction to American Catholic Magazines* (Philadelphia:
The American Catholic Historical Society of Philadelphia, 1952), p. 44.
[6] In *The Great Crisis in American Catholic History* (Chicago: Henry
Regnery Co., 1957), p. 117.

did aid in the conservation of the immigrant's faith. Indeed, whatever its weaknesses, it was quite impressive compared to the religious press of other denominations. Protestants themselves recognized this and made it a subject for discussion. Theodore L. Flood, for one, wrote in *The Chautauquan,* for March, 1895, that "the press of the Catholic Church is powerful, aggressive, and numerically strong," and he urged Protestants to imitate the Catholics, publish periodicals at a lower price, and thus increase opportunities for religious education of the poor.[7]

During the middle phase of its history, the period from 1900 through World War II, the Catholic press evolved pretty much as it is known today—multifaceted, and Church- controlled and -operated. The once common independent became a rarity, and there developed a dominance of the medium by an official diocesan newspaper press, and by a profusion of magazines sponsored in the main by religious orders but including fraternal and random publications of various origins.

There were several forces at work in this transition. The Catholic press of the late nineteenth century was in a bad state of overexpansion and duplication (the *American Newspaper Directory* for 1892 listed eight Catholic weeklies, one semiweekly and one German-Catholic weekly in New York, exclusive of Brooklyn), and hence it fell easy victim to a changing economy and to a broadening communications system which did away forever with the isolation not only of cities, but of communities within cities. The publication business became impossible for the less competitive, as well as for those who lacked capital. Thus scores of Catholic publications passed into oblivion. In the meanwhile, many bishops, acting in response to their own continuing exhortations for a robust and respectful Catholic press, either placed their authority behind a single publication whose policies they could control or trust, purchased an independent outright, or founded a publication of their own. This publication they then designated their official or semiofficial organ, and it proved an overwhelming

[7] *The Chautauquan,* XX, 728–29.

com petitor for the struggling independent. The independent gradually passed away; the Church-sponsored press waxed stronger and stronger.

This middle phase of the Catholic press in America was the time during which the Catholic press came to be a truly American Catholic press, a process to which numerous factors contributed, not the least of which were the loyalties stimulated by the Spanish-American War and World War I, and the shrinking absorption in Old World affairs as Ireland won its fight for freedom and Germany rattled sabers.

Also during this period, two giant national newspaper chains were born—*Our Sunday Visitor* and *The Register* chains. Though the temptation today in Catholic intellectual circles is to write off these publications, both have to be recognized for some effective apologetics (oldsters cite particularly *Our Sunday Visitor*'s refutations of *The Menace*, the Aurora, Missouri, weekly which for twenty years, beginning in 1911, carried on a campaign of hate and abuse against the Catholic Church). Likewise, both have to be credited for their service to whole areas of the United States, when without them there would have been nothing else. *Our Sunday Visitor* has been the official organ of twenty dioceses, and *The Register* of thirty-five. Ultimately, each diocese is largely responsible for the character of the paper it receives, since the home diocesan editor may write his own editorials and determine how he wants what news handled. We mention this merely to point up the fact that aside from the national editions, one cannot make a qualitative generalization about either chain as a whole. Each chain produces some weak papers, but each also produces some which hold their own in quite respectable company. The *Peoria Register* and the *Fort Wayne-South Bend Edition, Our Sunday Visitor,* are good examples of the latter.

The middle period saw, too, the founding of the National Catholic Welfare Conference News Service, an act which irrevocably committed the Church and the bishops in America to a Catholic press, and which removed the last stumbling block to wide and effective publication by making world-wide Catholic news as immediate and available to the tiniest diocese of the most meager assets as to the largest, most prosperous metropolitan see.

The N.C.W.C. News Service issued its first dispatches on April 11, 1920. Today it is the world's largest dispenser of Catholic news and information, serving more than 550 publications and radio stations in 65 countries. It has a network of 267 correspondents throughout the world, and forwards by teletype, telegram, and airmail news packet (principally) hundreds of thousands of words a year to subscribers; it also furnishes the complete texts of papal and Vatican documents, as well as other papers of importance. N.C.W.C. News Service is, in a word, the backbone of the Catholic press in the United States. Occasionally it seems to subscribing editors that NC (the service's date-line logotype abbreviation) is unnecessarily "diplomatic" or unduly deferential to the predilections of its 230 or so "bishop-bosses." But it is a first-class news service nonetheless, and it can boast of some distinguished correspondents, notably its Rome bureau chief, Msgr. James I. Tucek.

Many Catholic publications today supplement their NC coverage with that of Religious News Service, an affiliated but independently managed agency of the National Conference of Christians and Jews. RNS dates from 1934 and has been consistently reliable in its coverage of the non-Catholic as well as the Catholic world. Yet its recognition by the Catholic press was torturedly slow, perhaps because of old, deep-seated Catholic suspicion toward anything that smacked of interdenominationalism. In any case, there was resistance to RNS, and this was broken down only with the tardy recognition that RNS did not pose a threat to NC, that its excellence was impossible to ignore, and that it offered news in vast areas outside Catholicism, concerning which the Catholic editor should be acquainted and on which he was receiving little or nothing from specifically Catholic NC. Today, RNS supplies ninety Catholic publications; in 1945 the number was less than a third of that.

Finally, the middle period witnessed the founding in 1911 of the Catholic Press Association, a mutual-help organization whose purpose is to "assist members in publishing effective periodicals according to the demands of technical standards, and the truths of human reason and the Catholic Faith."[8] The association may not be vital, in the strict sense of the word, to the Catholic press, but it does provide its unifying bond. The unit efficiency and organization of the Catholic press of the 1960s is traceable in large part both to this association and to the men who headed it in the middle years, the great and the controversial, men like Simon A. Baldus of *Extension* (Chicago), Richard Reid of *The Catholic News* (New York), Vincent dePaul Fitzpatrick of the *Catholic Review* (Baltimore), Patrick F. Scanlan of the Brooklyn *Tablet*, Msgr. Peter M. H. Wynhoven of *Catholic Action of the South* (New Orleans), Alexander J. Wey of the *Catholic Universe Bulletin* (Cleveland), Humphrey E. Desmond of the *Catholic Herald Citizen* (Milwaukee), and many others. These were men who helped shape the history of Catholicism in America (some more constructively than others, to be sure), together with such priest-immortals of Catholic journalism as *Catholic World's* James W. Gillis, a Paulist, and *America's* Jesuit editors, Paul L. Blakely, John LaFarge, and Wilfrid Parsons.

Politically and socially, the Catholic press of this middle period failed to move Catholics appreciably beyond the isolated positions of the past. The loudest voices of the Catholic press were conservative and reactionary, and this fact no doubt explains at least partially the subsequent unblushing romance of so many Catholics with McCarthyism, and the furtive later flirtation of many with Birchism. It also helped stereotype an impression which lingers to this day in most non-Catholic and some Catholic quarters: that the Catholic press is dreary, negative, and contrary, combining "all the worst features of the bully and the martyr."[9]

The notion of a Catholic press boasting magazines and news-

[8] *1962 National Catholic Almanac*, ed. Felician A. Foy, O.F.M. (Paterson, N.J.: St. Anthony's Guild), p. 583.

[9] J. F. Powers, *Morte D'Urban* (New York: Doubleday & Company, Inc., 1962), p. 135.

papers which are topical, calm, thoughtful, and impartial has yet to occur to many apart from intimates of this press, just as it remains to be popularly recognized that the Catholic press can be other than the visual abortion it was during much of the middle period. Many of those who prejudge the Catholic press of the 1960s on its carry-over reputation from the 1920s and 1930s are amazed, upon introduction to the current product, to find frequent examples as newsy, bright, and stylish as the average secular publication of their acquaintance. This might mean much or little, of course, depending upon the reading tastes of the individual; but it does indicate that large sections of today's Catholic press compare in technique and presentation with their counterparts in the general press. In the middle period there was hardly any comparison between the two presses.

Culturally also, the performance of this "middle phase" Catholic press left much to be desired. Over the centuries the Catholic Church had won for itself a reputation as the great patron of learning and the arts; but little of this rubbed off on the Catholic press of the early twentieth century. Where the arts were concerned, the Catholic press coasted along sterile and uninspired.

The Catholic press, and with it American Catholics generally, had entered the twentieth century with no real cultural or intellectual tradition. As Msgr. John Tracy Ellis pointed out in his provocative analysis of the relationship of Catholics to American intellectual life, "the constant and heroic efforts of editors like Brownson in his *Quarterly Review,* of Hecker in the *Catholic World,* and of James A. Corcoran in the *American Catholic Quarterly Review,*" were unavailing in the nineteenth century in raising the intellectual interests of Catholics—even though their voices were complemented by the stirring pleas of bishops like John Lancaster Spalding of Peoria, and John Ireland of St. Paul. "The vast majority of Catholics remained relatively impervious to the intellectual movements of their time," Msgr. Ellis remarked.[10]

[10] *American Catholics and the Intellectual Life* (Chicago: Heritage Foundation, 1956), p. 24.

The correction of this condition could—indubitably should— have been a principal task of the Catholic press of the new century. Instead the Catholic press developed many of its least commendable qualities and grew dull and plodding. Matters reached such a state that, in one diocese, a once-great diocesan newspaper which had fallen on lean days was derisively tagged the diocesan fly swatter.

The third or modern stage in the evolution of the Catholic press came after World War II, when a whole body of bright young laymen repeopled editorial offices where laymen had been so prominent fifty and seventy-five years before, and wherein were enshrined the memories of editors of yesterday—O'Reilly, Roche, Pallen, Mosher, Egan, Desmond, Preuss, Donahue. A new breed became familiar, and new names emerged, from Anderson to Zens, and answering to McDonald, Hoyt, Murphy, O'Connor, Sherry, Thorman, Burns, Casserly, Quinn—the list is far from complete. These men brought with them the intelligent zeal of the great lay journalists of the nineteenth century; most possessed an early maturity honed by military service; some had experience in the daily press; and all claimed in common a confident, posi-tive outlook. They speedily transformed the Catholic press from an effort somewhat inordinately concerned with the saving of the saved, into a medium which peered beyond the altar railing and the convent wall and saw a world with which the Catholic press had to come firmly to grips. What laymen did for established but tired favorites, such as *The Sign, Ave Maria,* and *St. Jude,* and for infant publications such as the diocesan papers of Newark and Miami, was only slightly less than astonishing.

The first fruits of the toils of the post-World War II lay editors were primarily professional. Stories came to be tightly written; editorials were stripped of verbosity and their bite sharpened; make-up and picture displays brightened; news evaluations ma-tured; advertising grew more professional. Technically the Cath-olic press had moved at last beyond the amateur and semi-professional stages. And as it progressed, it extended its range of interests, at the same time eliminating heavy overlays of gabby institutionalism and editorial certitude for approaches more catholic and attitudes more flexible.

This is not to suggest that the hiring of laymen automatically solved all the problems of enlightened journalism for the Catholic press; some of the worst practices and products of this press today, in both the newspaper and magazine departments, are traceable to laymen.

Nor did the return of the layman harness all the impulses to wander into the extraneous. Some publications of lay (as well as clerical) influence are knee-deep in sideline businesses, such as travel and fund raising. Indeed, the use of the Catholic press for fund raising now enjoys such acceptance that a fund-raising conference was included in the Catholic Press Association's 1962 convention program. (Speakers discussed "Data Processing, Punch Cards, and Tape," "Appeals, Copy Content, and Packaging Promotion," and "Friends, Funds—Costs and Cares.")

Nor did the coming of the layman remove from the Catholic press as a whole all of the gross business practices that mushroomed with the circulation spiral of previous decades. The Catholic press is still glutted with insane and insipid advertising, and still embarrassed by questionable circulation procedures.

Whatever the reader's ailment, if he follows the advertising of the Catholic press he is almost certain to discover some promise for cure, whether the difficulty is falling hair, bunions, arthritis, piles, itches, constipation, slipping false teeth, a rupture, or bed wetting.

The irony is that publications which have no hesitancy about accepting suspicious medicine ads frequently display scruples about advertising they might legitimately carry. For instance, women's underwear and nylon stocking ads are frowned upon by many publications since they might shock the sensibilities, not of men, but of the very people who wear these items—and, in all likelihood, wear them because of an advertisement read without offense in the general press.

But actually this is a minor complaint. A more serious criticism of the advertising in the Catholic press concerns the so-called religious-goods ads. These are sometimes in unbelievable taste: "The Talking 'Lady of Fatima Doll' . . . Bringing you the loving message of Fatima, accompanied by soft, sacred musical background"; the "Beautiful Bust of Christ with Miracle-of-the-Sun Halo . . . brilliant when struck by sunlight—mysteriously bright when displayed near a window on a dull, overcast day"; and "Costumes to Inspire Your Little Boy or Girl. Watch how they will assume the quiet dignity of those who have dedicated their lives to the Church. This fine imaginative play will help them plan their lives . . . the Catholic Way. Little Nun $8.95; Little Priest $8.95."

What makes the grossness of such material in the Catholic press all the more inexcusable is the fact that in 1955 members of the Catholic Press Association pledged themselves to a "Code of Fair Publishing Practices," one article of which declared: "We will not publish advertisements of products whose ordinary purpose or use makes Catholic devotion primarily a matter of sentiment rather than of intellectual faith, or whose copy states, suggests or implies that Catholic devotion is primarily sentimental."

Often enough, it is publications of religious orders which run such tasteless ads. In contrast, it is not infrequently the lay-directed journal which exhibits taste. For example, editor Edward Rice of *Jubilee* has been known to discontinue a religious order's advertisement of its annuity program because he considered the copy misleading and thought the annuity plan took advantage of people under the guise of good works; this same ad can be found in almost any diocesan newspaper. *Jubilee* has also refused vocation ads deemed insipid or derogatory toward Protestants, as well as ads for switch-blade knives and Elvis Presley records which large, nationally circulated, priest-edited magazines willingly accepted. But high purpose is not always rewarded. Most diocesan newspapers are doing quite well, and the magazines that carried the switch-blade knife and Elvis Presley record ads are publications of great affluence; *Jubilee* is living almost from hand to mouth.

In the matter of circulation, so many publications, particularly diocesan newspapers, depend on quota systems, school subscription crusades, and complete parish coverage plans (the *Long Island Catholic* was born May 3, 1962, with a circulation of 208,000), the impression is created that the Catholic press is not nearly so popular among Catholics as the circulation totals would seem to indicate, but rather that it is rammed down the throats of vast numbers of the reluctant. This feeling strengthens as one sees garbed religious, male and female, pushing doorbells and volunteering as parish census-takers in order to sell their Order's products.

Unquestionably, if Catholic publications were sold wholly on their merit, and not on secondary grounds of loyalty, of promoting an apostolate or supporting missions, Catholic press circulation figures would shrink considerably. By the same token, there would be considerably fewer than 501 Catholic magazines and newspapers. Deprived of built-in pressures and contrived promotion schemes, many would fade rapidly into oblivion.

This would hardly amount to a disaster, if it meant a diminishing of the mediocrity that gluts the Catholic market. A rationale can be advanced for the diocesan press numbering as many newspapers as it does (a "one diocese, one paper" sort of logic). But it is not so easy to defend the proliferation of Catholic magazines, especially in light of the undistinguished and overlapping performance of so many of them. Unwittingly these publications often do a double disservice: they stifle intelligent reader interest in the Catholic press as a whole, and they drain off from more worthy publications advertising and subscription income which could be put to much better advantage. It is a great pity when estimable publications like *The Commonweal, Jubilee,* and *The Critic,* all three selling squarely on their merits, have to do gymnastics to balance their account books, while second-rate publications with access to church pulpits, organization membership files, or parish census cards grow fatter, wealthier, and more comfortable. It is almost enough to make one pray for the coming to pass of Dan Herr's quip: "There is nothing basically wrong with the Catholic

press in America that an acute paper shortage would not cure."[11]
The trouble is that since Catholic reading habits are what they
are, a paper shortage would likely mow down the good publications and leave the mediocre to continue their commonplace
service.

THE CATHOLIC PRESS
AND THE AMERICAN SCENE

Except for fleeting moments, the American Catholic press has
seldom regarded itself as other than supplementary to the American general press, providing a special witness focusing on the
dimension of religion in the news, and presenting reports, articles,
and instruction understandably not to be found in a press serving
a pluralistic society.

The generally fair and impartial nature of the secular press is
undoubtedly one reason why the Catholic press could conveniently confine itself to auxiliary status with limited schedules of
weekly or monthly publication. Despite occasional ruptures
(such as the insulting 1870 coverage of Vatican Council I in
which, for instance, The New York Herald referred to the Holy
See as an "edifice of folly" and The Nation labeled Pius IX
"simple-minded"), the Catholic Church in America has never
had to contend with a general press which was consistently or
aggressively anticlerical, secularist, or revolutionary in spirit.
Hence it escaped the alternative of its press becoming a competitor to the general press in anything resembling the sense in
which the Catholic press of Europe was forced to be in the
nineteenth century. (Two of Europe's most influential Catholic
dailies of today, l'Osservatore Romano and La Croix, were born
in Italy and France, respectively, of the very challenges the
Church in America was spared.)

There were other factors, of course, in the determination of
the Catholic press in America as a periodical rather than a daily

[11] Dan Herr, Stop Pushing! (New York: Doubleday/Hanover House,
1961), p. 159.

competitive press, not the least of which was the constitutionally benign attitude of government. Apart from the Know-Nothing phenomenon of the mid-1800s, and then only in a few states, Catholics were never faced with hostilities which were officially governmental. As the Catholic bishops pointed out in their annual statement of 1962, strengths and advantages accrued to the Church "from living and growing in an atmosphere of religious and political freedom."[12] This does not mean that the Church in America achieved its maturity in an environment that was always friendly and sympathetic to its aspirations; but it does mean that the situation was never such that the Church was required to make a political or religious forum out of its press.

Nor was it necessary for Catholics to be apprehensive toward government or the general press in connection with indoctrination in any prevailing cult. Government in America might once have been disposed toward Protestantism, but it has always been officially nonpartisan; likewise the general press might once have been strongly Protestant-oriented, but in practice it has still maintained a nondenominational personality. The Catholic Church in America entertained great anxieties over the Protestant nature of the public school system, and this was a consideration in the Church's evolving of a substitute school system of its own. But anxieties in other directions were never so strong that it became imperative to establish substitute newspapers or a daily Catholic press. (To be sure, the Catholic press's magazine section includes branches which are in no wise auxiliary or supplementary to the secular press. But these, however important, are specialty publications—journals of opinion, scholarly quarterlies, learned reviews, mission and devotional magazines, and so on.)

Despite the congenial circumstances of life in America, the possibility of an expanded Catholic press competing from day to day with the general press is one that has occurred from time to time, beginning first with Fr. Isaac Hecker's unsuccessful attempt

[12] *Statement on the Ecumenical Council,* issued by the Administration Board of the National Catholic Welfare Conference on behalf of the cardinals, archbishops, and bishops of the United States, August, 1962.

to raise $300,000 in 1871 to purchase a New York daily newspaper then for sale. But only at the Third Plenary Council of Baltimore, which the American bishops convened in 1884, was the possibility seriously broached on the level of broad Church policy. This developed when the bishops adopted a decree stating:

> It is greatly to be desired that in some of our large cities a Catholic daily newspaper be maintained fully equal to the secular daily newspapers in financial strength and the sagacity, vigor and authority of its writers. Nor is it necessary that the word Catholic be displayed at the head of its pages. It is sufficient that in addition to current events, and all those things which in other daily newspapers are eagerly desired, it defend, whenever a proper opportunity presents itself, the Catholic Church from assaults and calumnies of its enemies, and explain its doctrine; and, moreover, that it carefully abstain from placing before its readers anything that is scandalous or unbecoming.[13]

The action of the bishops is understandable both in terms of the tensions for the Church in Europe (it had been only three years since it was necessary to carry out the reburial of Pius IX at nighttime; even so his coffin was splattered with the mud of anticlericals[14]), and in terms of their own experience with excesses in America (suspicions against immigrants, of whom Catholics comprised the vast majority, were such that as late as 1892 the Populist party hammered together a platform, one plank of which emphasized "the fallacy of protecting American labor under the present system, which opens our ports to the pauper and criminal classes of the world"[15]). But if the fears of the American bishops for the future were shared generally, there was no evidence of it in a rush to set up a Catholic daily press. Catho-

[13] Third Plenary Council of Baltimore, Title vii, No. 227, para. 2.
[14] E. E. Y. Hales, *Pio Nono* (New York: Doubleday/Image Books, 1962), p. 347.
[15] *The American Story*, ed. Earl Schenck Miers (Manhasset, N.Y.: Channel Press, Inc., 1956), p. 244.

lics remained calm, seemed satisfied with the general daily press and little disposed to build a competitive press of their own.

There were, though, isolated exceptions. In 1904 an attempt was made in Buffalo to implement the decree of the Third Plenary Council, when the owners of a German-language daily proposed to convert their newspaper to a Catholic, English-language daily. Despite the backing of the bishop of Buffalo and the support of the clergy, however, the publishers could raise only $31,600 toward a $100,000 launching fund, and the project had to be abandoned. Indifference of the laity was widespread.

A similar attitude also helped account for the demise of the Catholic daily which appeared in Dubuque, Iowa, from 1920 to 1942 (almost always struggling, and with a circulation which peaked in 1937 with 21,000 but which averaged out at 14,000). It was also a factor in the brief career (142 issues) of *The Sun Herald*, the post-World War II attempt of a zealous group of young laymen, under the editorship of Robert G. Hoyt, to create a national Catholic daily.

A touch of irony is added to the *Sun Herald* story when it is examined in the light of the 1884 encouragement of the American bishops. Originally it was the intention to publish this Catholic daily out of Chicago (under the name *The Morning Star*); however, the project was opposed there in 1949 by some of the parties to whom in 1884 laymen would have looked for patronage. Mr. Hoyt writes of the incident thus in the *Catholic Press Annual '61:*

> Then one day came a telephone call from the Chancery Office, informing us that we were ordered under pain of sin to suspend any effort to publish the paper in the Chicago Archdiocese—and that if we persisted in defiance of this order the paper would be denounced from every pulpit.
>
> We asked and obtained an audience with Cardinal Stritch, but his decision stood. I don't recall that we ever learned the ultimate basis for the decision, but my impression is that he didn't think there could be a paper staffed by Catholics, known to be attempting a Catholic interpretation of events, which

would yet not involve the Church. No doubt he also had reservations about the professional and educational qualifications of the group. Anyway, we were out.

The episode not only dramatized how changed were the times and the attitude toward a Catholic daily press from those which existed in 1884; it also reinforced the theory of those who argued that the long-standing indifference of Catholics toward a daily Catholic press was nothing over which to brood.

The need for a Catholic daily press was never crystal clear; more importantly, its desirability was always questionable. Aside from the doubtful public relations connected with any real or imagined polarization of talent, subscriptions, and advertisers, the challenge for Catholics seemed to rest instead in supporting and influencing positively that area of journalism where greater good stood to be accomplished—the general press. A Catholic daily press, had it evolved, would assuredly have been superfluous; if one had developed on any wide scale, it could easily have made ghetto walls even harder to tear down; and almost surely, such a Catholic daily press would have been caught in the economic squeeze which between 1909 and 1961 forced 837 daily newspapers in the United States to go out of business.[16] The indifference of Catholic readers toward a Catholic daily press, therefore, appears to have been a blessing in disguise. It may be that the Chicago Chancery Office also felt thus when it talked with Mr. Hoyt.

One last word about the alleged need of a Catholic daily press. The strongest refutation to such a need is to be found not in historical or statistical projection, but in the performance of the very person who dedicated so much of his talent and his time toward the establishment of a Catholic daily, Robert Hoyt. For if Mr. Hoyt's present editorship of *The Catholic Reporter*, the weekly publication of the Diocese of Kansas City-St. Joseph, Missouri, makes anything perfectly clear, it is that a perceptive

[16] Cf. A. J. Liebling, *The Press* (New York: Ballantine Books, Inc., 1961), p. 16.

and imaginative Catholic weekly can do most, if not all, of what a Catholic daily might be expected to do.

However, not everyone is prepared to agree with these conclusions. As recently as the summer of 1962, the executive editor of the *Catholic Star Herald* of Camden, New Jersey, Very Rev. Salvatore J. Adamo, was polling other Catholic editors on the feasibility of launching a Catholic daily newspaper. The dream refuses to vaporize.

Of course, one of the things that keeps the candle of hope flickering for dreamers of a Catholic daily press is *The Christian Science Monitor,* a top-flight newspaper which is not superfluous, which neither builds ghetto walls nor isolates Christian Scientists. But for the Catholic press to come up with anything similar, it would need two blessings without which the *Monitor* would be a quite different newspaper: subsidy and assurance of full support. Subsidy is relatively easy to conceive of, but support is something else entirely. As clergy-Catholic press relationships are presently constituted in America, it is difficult to picture a Catholic daily press which could count on the patronage of succeeding bishops without at the same time becoming subject to clerical controls.

Although the Catholic press has settled on what amounts to an auxiliary function, at least so far as daily journalism is concerned, nonetheless it has been able to perform memorable service to Church and country by bearing witness to truth in areas which were passed over in silence or misunderstood on other levels of American journalism. Cases in point would be its calling attention to the religious persecution in Mexico in the 1920s, and its unrelenting focus on the crusading atheism of world communism at a time when the focus of the general press was on the political, economic, and military aspects of the system. This holds true, even though many Catholic publications were so caught up by anticommunism hysteria that the service rendered came close to being totally neutralized.

Then, too, there was the performance of the Catholic press in the 1960 Presidential campaign, when Catholic newspapers and journals of opinion, while maintaining a strict and honorable impartiality, lived up to their potential, both editorially and reportorially, making a substantial contribution to a healthier political climate.

In the realm of party politics, incidentally, the Catholic press is today rather carefully nonpartisan. It might take a position on issues, but it conscientiously abstains from involvement in candidacies or parties. Some Catholic publications accept political advertising, but others spurn it, seeing in political advertising a possible compromise to impartiality, or being unconvinced that political advertising makes any great contribution to clarity of issues under debate or to appraisal of the candidates themselves.

Despite its real contributions, the Catholic press nevertheless has often defaulted leadership in areas which should have commended themselves naturally to the Catholic conscience and concern. This retreat or abstention from responsibility is nothing recent; indeed, it is chronic. Going back to the nineteenth century and its turbulent times of social reform, Jesuit historian Lucey has noted that it took the *American Ecclesiastical Review* until Volume V to make its first reference to labor, after changing name (from *The Pastor*) in January, 1889, and broadening scope: "The relatively few references to labor and labor unions would seem to indicate that this was not an urgent problem to the clergy during these years."[17]

Obviously it was not a matter of pressing concern to the Catholic reading public either, if one is allowed a judgment on the experience of the *New Carmelite Review,* a periodical attempted in Chicago during the early century and dedicated to discussion of political, economic, and social questions. The *New Carmelite Review* was inspired, however belatedly, by Leo XIII's "Rerum Novarum," and was carefully designed to meet a need among American Catholics. However, the *Review* could survive only from November 1903, to June 1904. Fr. Lucey observed: "The failure is a commentary on the attitudes of Catholics towards the

[17] *An Introduction to American Catholic Magazines, op. cit.,* pp. 25–26.

practical application of Catholic principles to current social problems."[18]

Even the esteemed Jesuit journal of opinion, *America*, established in 1909 to "give information and suggest principles that may help to the solution of the vital problems constantly thrust upon our people,"[19] could not escape, at least for a time, the drifts of detachment. Looking back on the magazine's first fifty years, and evaluating *America's* performance on the tariff and tax questions of its early days, Fr. Benjamin L. Masse, S.J., remarked: "Week after week *America* chronicled the course of the debate, but so soberly and objectively did the editors perform this chore that it is difficult today to know where their sympathies lay. Perhaps, like the Catholic community, whose interests and concerns they mirrored, they hadn't yet charted a course through the swirling currents of early 20th Century opinion. By that time the riches of Leo XIII's 'Rerum Novarum' . . . had barely been scratched."[20]

But matters improved. They would have had to—if not in direct response to papal pronouncements, then from the prodding of documents such as the 1919 "Bishops' Program of Social Reconstruction," and the brilliant examples of priests like Fr. John A. Ryan, a prophetic voice in the field, and of laymen like Philip Murray of the CIO and the Steelworkers Union—the latter so representative of a type of Catholic layman with social attitudes instinctively in the tradition of papal instructions, and far ahead of corresponding positions in the American Catholic press.

Of course, not all Catholic publications stood back in those years from the reality of social reform. Some—like Chicago's *New World*, the *Michigan Catholic*, the *Pittsburgh Catholic*, San Francisco's *Monitor*, the *St. Louis Watchman*, and surprisingly enough to a later generation, *The Wanderer*—spoke loudly and clearly on the minimum wage, collective bargaining, social

[18] *Ibid.*, p. 65.

[19] Editorial Announcement, *America*, Vol. 1, No. 1, April 17, 1909.

[20] Benjamin L. Masse, "A Half-Century of Social Action," *America*, April 11, 1959.

security, and other issues affecting the rights of the worker and the dignity of the individual. But they spoke almost from quarantine, and to relatively small audiences. In typical fashion, the bulk of the Catholic press was locked in the towers of theory when the times called for involvement and application. It was the old story of entanglement in premises, and delay in conclusions—a penchant still so much a part of the Catholic character that Pope John XXIII might have had it in mind when in "Mater et Magistra" he pleaded with Catholics "not [to] exhaust themselves in interminable discussions and, under the pretext of the better or the best, abstain from doing the good that is possible and thus obligatory" (paragraph 238).

The Catholic press of the 1960s may still be weak in delineating local application of social doctrine, yet it is considerably more conscious of the over-all social question than its counterpart of a few decades ago. In fact, Fr. Robert Graham, S.J., in evaluating press reaction to "Mater et Magistra," found that "notwithstanding the often quite generous space given [in modern times by the secular press] to papal statements and viewpoints, the Catholic press showed its coverage was unique and indispensable."[21]

This statement should not be used as grounds for total consolation. The Catholic press has traditionally reacted in full potential to something as obvious as a papal social encylical; anything else would be inexcusable, especially when, as in the case of "Mater," its coming and importance were heralded months beforehand.

Unfortunately, on issues more obscure than a papal encyclical, this is not always the case, and the Catholic press often appears indolent and indecisive. Hence one witnessed in Pennsylvania, in 1960–61, much of that state's Catholic press relinquishing to a labor union (the United Steelworkers of America) responsibility which should have been shared in championing a fair-housing-practices law.

Similarly, the echo from the Catholic press of the democracy of

21 *America,* August 26, 1961.

the Church on racial matters has been considerably less than resonant. In addition, there is the paradox that where racial problems are the more complex and sensitive, there the echo is often the fainter or absent altogether. After the rioting (Sunday, September 30, 1962) which accompanied the integration of the University of Mississippi, a surveyer of ninety diocesan newspapers for the following Friday found that fifty-six (almost two-thirds) did not treat of the incident, despite the fact that this was "a crisis that would seem to demand commitment by Catholic editors, a crisis that would call for blunt editorial denunciation of the evil forces of racism."[22] The majority of Catholic editorial writers were wishing "Bon Voyage to the Bishop" as he left for the Second Vatican Council, calling for prayers for the council (admittedly a "must" editorial theme), scoring communism in Cuba, urging registration for the November elections, and deploring the visit of the Secretary of the Interior to Russia. The surveyer also found an editorial saluting organists and choir members on National Choir Recognition Day, October 7.

A quiet—heavy though not complete—also hangs over such urgent topics as peace and disarmament, themes which are of the very essence of Christianity. The cries from the Catholic press are shrill when the military rights or securities of the native land or the free world are neglected or intruded upon, but the work of the peacemaker is left to the obscure government official, the Catholic Association for International Peace, and the disciples of Dorothy Day. As a test of this observation, it would be interesting to be able to learn how many readers of the Catholic press know of the work (indeed of the existence) of the United States Arms Control and Disarmament Agency, through their Catholic newspaper or magazine; they would be precious few. ("Pacem in Terris," Pope John's "peace on earth" encyclical of April 11, 1963, should alter attitudes, however.)

Phenomena like these provide potent ammunition for those critics quick to write the Catholic press off as studiously circum-

[22] Dan Herr, "Stop Pushing!" *The Critic*, December 1962–January 1963.

spect, and as a medium which reflects rather than helps fashion the religious and moral values of the community.

The pattern repeats itself in other fields. In civil liberties, for instance, Dean Joseph O'Meara, Jr., of the College of Law, Notre Dame University, has noted that "for some reason Catholics in the United States as a group don't seem to really understand the connection between their rights and the rights of every other man in our nation."[23] Actually, the reason is not nearly so mysterious as implied; it can be explained at least partially by the almost habitual disinclination of the Catholic press to fret about injustices other than those imperiling Catholics or specifically Catholic interests. Bigotry is deplored when the one discriminated against is Catholic; bias in the administration of zoning ordinances is denounced when the rights being violated belong to Catholics. The same is seldom true when bigotry is directed against Jews, or when there is opposition to the construction plans of, say, a Lutheran parish.

By the same token, the Catholic press frequently approaches with reserve "family" affairs which one expects would be treated boldly and candidly in the "family" press above all others. One thinks back to the reporting of the first session of Vatican Council II (October 11—December 8, 1962). Many spokesmen congratulated the Catholic press on its coverage; however, it was embarrassingly obvious that the Catholic press's cautious coverage was second-best to that by large sections of the Protestant and secular presses. More specifically, apart from the Gregory Baum articles in *The Commonweal* and the Claud Nelson–Robert Graham reporting for Religious News Service, there was very little in the Catholic press during those months that compared with "Xavier Rynne's" reports from Vatican City in *The New Yorker* (surprisingly enough), or with Harold E. Fey's coverage in *The Christian Century*, an undenominational but Protestant weekly. The Catholic Press Association presented a special cita-

[23] Interview with Donald J. Thorman, *Voice of St. Jude,* December 1960; republished in pamphlet form by the American Freedoms Council, now the Catholic Council on Civil Liberties, Hamburg, N.Y.

tion, at its 1963 convention in Miami, to *The New Yorker* for its coverage.

One could extend observations of this sort into a litany of criticism by examining the performance of the Catholic press in areas of community life, particularly prior to 1945. But it is a disservice to the improved Catholic press of today to dwell on the shortcomings of yesterday. More and more civic and social action subjects, which once would have been treated by the Catholic press in retrospect, are topics of early and timely attention, when policies and procedures admit of shaping and when involvement counts. This is an important point, for it is evidence that the Catholic press is increasingly aware of the effective role it can play in the world of men.

Of course, much more could and should be done; no one would contend otherwise. But to do all that needs doing will require staffs much larger than those presently engaged by the average Catholic publication. *America* magazine counts twelve full-time editors and twenty-two corresponding editors, but how many other Catholic publications enjoy the luxury of a staff half that size? Most struggle along with three, four, or five editorial staffers, and this number of people can do only so much.

Diocesan newspapers especially, it must be recognized, are seriously understaffed; and if the individual publication is ever to increase the degree and effectiveness of its community-reporting activity, this manpower shortage must be relieved. There is hardly a diocesan paper which could not use to advantage one or two topnotch men reporting and interpreting the local scene. Most Catholic newspapers have their copy editor, their society editor, and sports editor, all of them busily employed handling departmental assignments. How many papers, on the other hand, can claim a reporter whose job it is to specialize in the much more important areas of social action and community or civic affairs?

The workers in the Catholic press appreciate the need for more and greater depth reporting, and this helps explain the founding in 1961, by eight or so diocesan newspapers, of the Catholic

Features Cooperative, a group which pools a weekly sum and draws on this to commission articles which the single publication could not afford. This group has grown to twelve (the agreed maximum) and it has tapped worth-while sources that would have gone untouched. But the cooperative has merely eased the national and international depth-reporting problem of its dozen members; still distressing is the problem of the local level—for these twelve and most others besides.

THE CATHOLIC PRESS AND PUBLIC OPINION

Several questions provoked by the increasing presence of the laity in the Catholic press are just now beginning to come into focus as the bishops and priests who made the initial commitment to the laity pass on to other sees, other responsibilities, or other worlds. What changes will occur under a new bishop or priest-adviser? Will continuity of conviction be allowed the lay editor, or must, for example, an editor of liberal outlook be required to reshape his political and social philosophy to fit, say, the more reserved or conservative viewpoints of a new ecclesiastical superior? The subject ultimately expands to how free should the Catholic press be from the ruling ecclesiastical authority, how independent should the editor be, and what should be his role in evolving public opinion? Obviously, as the topic expands, it involves the priest- or religious-editor as well.

The matter of commitment to the lay editors is of primary concern both to those thinking of entering the Catholic press, and to those already at work in it. Until a couple of years ago this was merely a speculative anxiety, but the unhappy experience of laymen in several sees, when clerical realignments touched their papers, dramatized how real was (or is) this worry. Unquestionably, it deters the entrance into Catholic journalism of articulate laymen who feel they have something to say but who suspect that one day they may be inhibited in expression; at the same time the situation causes many active Catholic lay journalists,

especially among the younger men still in secondary roles of
employ, to be receptive to opportunities outside the Catholic
press.

The lay Catholic journalist, like anyone else, can be comfortable as long as he is dealing with a known quantity, but in his
case there is no guarantee the known quantity will be around after
the next appointment list is issued from the Apostolic Delegation,
Chancery, or Provincial Headquarters. In this respect the Catholic editor, whether layman or cleric, is in a position comparable
to his counterpart in the general press, who can be hired and
fired, silenced and dispatched at the whim of a publisher or a
board of directors (and often as not is, when the publication
changes ownership). The Catholic editor wonders, though,
whether he might not escape this occupational hazard of his
counterpart at least partially, if only because in his case the so-
called "great question" has already been settled by a profound
agreement between employer and employee on the basic assumptions about man, his origin and destiny, his spiritual nature
and corresponding responsibilities. It goes without saying that in
the general press, agreement of this kind between editor and publisher could not be presumed.

In his aspiration, the editor is neither overbearing nor one-
sided. No Catholic editor argues that his rights are absolute, and
all recognize that there are definite obligations to satisfy the
publisher, and at the same time to represent the people by providing, if not what readers want, at least what a mature wisdom
suggests is best for them.

In going about this task the Catholic editor, and specifically the
layman, would find it consoling if a set of ground rules existed,
and also if there were some sort of warranty that ecclesiastical
appointment of clerics to posts entailing editorial supervision,
immediate or remote, would somehow be buttressed with in-
fusions of editorial wisdom. The lay journalist could then go
about his duties with one less neurosis in his unconscious. But
unfortunately this is not the way of the Church Militant. There

are no ground rules, and the interest, importance, and interpretation which bishops and religious superiors place on the
Catholic press vary from man to man, appointment to appointment. Further, the first experience many of these often have
with editorial regency comes with their selection for larger office—which probably explains the incongruity of assigning to
positions of direct editorial responsibility clerics whose credentials
are based on the writing of good term papers in seminary, a
journalism course in Sophomore B, or some equal irrelevancy.

One can count on two hands (if not one), those priests active
in Catholic journalism who have special training to qualify them
for their work.

But presuming a continued commitment of the Catholic press
to the professional Catholic lay journalist ι the growth of the
Catholic press and the shortage of vocations for religious are
such that anything else is virtually unthinkable), the question of
editorial freedom is still unresolved. This is a knotty problem,
and one whose solution is neither elementary nor to be soon
anticipated; for it is not a matter which can be settled by decree
or by arriving at agreement as to when whose rights supersede or
intrude upon whose privileges. The solution depends, rather, upon
an intellectual climate considerably different from that which exists
today in the Church in America, a climate much more reflective
of the attitude of Pius XII as expressed in his 1950 address to the
International Congress of the Catholic Press. Pius XII declared that
since the Church is a living body, "something would be lacking
in her life if she were deficient in public opinion and if this lack
were attributable to her pastors and faithful." In this context he
advised the Catholic journalist to guard against mute servility
and uncontrolled criticism, as well as the extremes of unreal and
illusory spiritualism, and a defeatist and materialistic realism, in
order that the Catholic press might "exercise its influence on public opinion within the Church, in the midst of the faithful." "Only
thus," Pope Pius concluded, "can be avoided false ideas on the
mission and possibilities of the Church in temporal matters, and,

especially today, on the social question and the problem of peace."[24]

Anyone who has done even minimal reading in the Catholic press knows that on nondoctrinal subjects there is no lack of public opinion in the pages of Catholic publications. The trouble is, there is so tight a closing of ranks on sensitive issues that a tendency develops to minimize, or to view cynically, the public discussion which goes on regularly. Some contend that it is one thing for the conservative and liberal wings of the Catholic press to whale away at each other, and for Catholic publications to debate passionately over fallout shelter ethics, the performance of the President, or the football policies of Notre Dame. This is innocent enough; it involves secondary issues and does not touch the hierarchy or sacrosanct policies and institutions. One is tempted to think twice about referring to "sacrosanct institutions" after the strong criticism one of the most sacrosanct of these, the Catholic University of America, received in the Catholic press for scratching four prominent theologians[25] from consideration as speakers in a 1963 campus lecture series. However, the barring of the theologians was a blunder so egregious that the incident qualified as an exception to the usual rules of reporting. It would have been a journalistic perversion to have let the matter pass in silence. Even so, not the whole Catholic press was outspoken on the barring; a number observed an editorial silence, and some slapped a total news embargo on the affair as well. Still, the fact that some Catholic publications could report the incident fully and in its total implication—*The Oklahoma Courier* and the *Steubenville Register* were especially forthright (the latter not always judicious)—indicates that inhibitions have been relieved. Nevertheless, it does not mean that the Catholic press can "free wheel" as it chooses. There are still sacred grounds and one

[24] *The Pope Speaks,* ed. Michael Chinigo (New York: Pantheon Books, Inc., 1957), pp. 357–58.

[25] Fr. John Courtney Murray, S.J., and Fr. Gustave Weigel, S.J., both of Woodstock (Md.) College, a Jesuit seminary; Fr. Godfrey Diekmann, O.S.B., editor of *Worship* magazine; and Fr. Hans Kueng of the University of Tuebingen, Germany.

does not tread on these without risking the fury, both from within and without the Catholic press, that greeted *The Commonweal*'s objections[26] to the manner in which the American bishops appeared to conduct their 1961 campaign for federal aid to parochial schools.

For its forthrightness in declaring that the American bishops spurned the role "of persuasive spokesmen for the Catholic community" and "cast themselves as a minority pressure group, trying to win special legislation by strategic, balance-of-power influence on legislation involving the general welfare,"[27] *The Commonweal* was labeled "a Pontius Pilate" by columnist Martin L. Duggan of the *Catholic Messenger* of Davenport, Iowa. Duggan charged that *The Commonweal* was "willing to wash its hands of all American Catholic children, while pretending to be the great and true friend of education."[28] Lining up with him, Dale Francis, in his *Our Sunday Visitor* column, scored *The Commonweal*'s "almost insolent confidence," and added that it was as if *The Commonweal*'s editors "know better what is good for the Church and the country than does the Hierarchy."[29] (*The Commonweal*'s position was to urge Catholic support of a federal aid to education bill while, at the same time, it asked non-Catholics to give greater attention to the needs of parochial schools.)

Predictably, there were reactions from the hierarchy. One rebuked "certain laymen" for "ignorant, insolent and arrogant criticism of the Bishops of the country,"[30] (*The Pilot* of Boston whimsically headed its coverage of the story: "Laity Be Good"). Another admonished that the job of Catholic lay leaders is to carry out the teachings of the Church and not to yield to any temptations "to tell the Church what it should be teaching."[31] The

[26] *The Commonweal*, Feb. 23, 1962, and March 23, 1962.

[27] *Ibid.*, Feb. 23, 1962.

[28] *Catholic Messenger*, March 5, 1962.

[29] *Our Sunday Visitor*, May 13, 1962.

[30] Bishop George W. Ahr of Trenton, in an address to the Ancient Order of Hibernians, April 23, 1962, in Trenton; as reported by N.C.W.C. News Service.

[31] Archbishop Joseph T. McGucken of San Francisco, in his enthronement sermon, April 3, 1962, in St. Mary's Cathedral, San Francisco.

cautions of the bishops were not pinpointed and the frame of reference may have been larger than what this writer interpreted it to be, a possibility which must be allowed in view of earlier "anti-layism" observations by Gerard E. Sherry when he was managing editor of the *Central California Register*. At least two weeks before *The Commonweal's* first editorial on the federal-aid campaign subject, Mr. Sherry spoke in Fresno of "a deep-seated suspicion on the part of some of the clergy against any interference by the laity."[32] It could be, therefore, that the episcopal protests cited stemmed from incidents unrelated to the federal-aid controversy and belonging to another reference, but this deduction appears sanguine.

Let it be noted that in the dispute in question strong clerical voices rose to defend *The Commonweal* and the layman's right of public expression. The priest-edited Indianapolis *Criterion* defended *The Commonweal's* right to "legitimate expression of lay opinion on a public issue" since "after all, the Federal Aid to Education bill is not a matter of faith or morals."[33] The Boston *Pilot's* priest-columnist, Msgr. George W. Casey, spoke in more general terms: "What . . . most people who are appalled at the de-Christianization of society think is most needed on the part of the laity is enthusiasm, initiative, leadership and participation, not submission and the passive virtues."[34] And Richard Cardinal Cushing of Boston, addressing the 1962 convention of the Catholic Press Association, offered this endorsement:

> I am proud to say that they [the laity] have already proven themselves [in the Catholic press] and in this way have brought our press to its present greatness. But I must say even more. In making this contribution to the Catholic press they have contributed to the Church as a whole, because what they have done in one apostolate, their success will encourage others to do in the thousand apostolates that lie before us. As

[32] As reported by Religious News Service, Feb. 8, 1962, p. 12.
[33] March 16, 1962.
[34] "Driftwood" column, May 12, 1962.

the age of the layman comes into being, it is no small thing to have been among the first to show the way. Generations will look back upon these days and upon your work, and, like the Lord Himself, they will call it good.

But in spite of such testimonials, the laity of the Catholic press is still inclined to view skeptically the authenticity and the actual extent of the commitment to them and their editorial authority. Whatever the protestations to the contrary, when conflict arises involving the will of the hierarchy and the disposition of the Catholic press, the laity suspects that the shepherds-and-the-sheep ethos will prevail. The aid to education case gives them a strong supporting argument, for although there were several possible positions on this question (one member of the hierarchy was reported as saying he could think of five),[35] it was not the several possible positions, but the position of the dominant voices of the American hierarchy which was conveyed to the American public as the official position of the Catholic Church. Columnist Donald McDonald quoted a non-Catholic editor in describing this as the "obstructionist" position—unless Catholics were counted in, everybody would be counted out.[36] (Attitudes and tactics changed drastically by 1963; even *The Commonweal* [March 15, 1963] was gratified by the calm and moderation with which the "Catholic case" was being advanced.)

The initial question, therefore, about the rights of the lay editor to "tenure" and to continuity of editorial position in the face of episcopal or clerical change, leads to another, larger area of concern: What should be the role of the Catholic press in America in stimulating public opinion within the Church? Of course the Catholic press is expected to be submissive to the hierarchy, the teaching Church, on doctrinal matters, but must it be subservient on the nondoctrinal as well? Is it to be allowed to excite and reflect public opinion on peripheral issues, and then be

[35] Bishop John J. Wright of Pittsburgh, as cited by Donald McDonald in his syndicated column of June 28, 1962.
[36] *Loc. cit.*

relegated to the role of publicist or propagandist on issues about which the episcopacy has reached a prior judgment?

Or is it to stir frank exchange so that, as Fr. Karl Rahner suggests,[37] the Church might adapt the more conveniently and effectively to the extraordinarily varied and many-sided contemporary conditions that affect it as a society of human beings? Fr. Rahner's advice in this regard could beneficially be framed on many walls: "If they [the clergy] do not allow the people to speak their minds, do not, in more dignified language, encourage or even tolerate, with courage and forbearance and even a certain optimism free from anxiety, the growth of public opinion within the Church, they run the risk of directing her from a soundproof ivory tower, instead of straining their ears to catch the voice of God, which can also be audible within the clamour of the times . . ."[38]

It is my conviction that the role of the laity in the Catholic press—indeed, the role of the clerical editor and of the Catholic press itself—will not and cannot be satisfactorily determined until it is first agreed *what the Catholic press is.* One would expect such an understanding to be basic, not merely to discussion about responsibilities and privileges, but to the week-to-week, month-to-month operation of the press itself. Instead, it is unenunciated and actually of fluctuating (if that) concern.

With few exceptions, Catholic newspapers are "official" publications of a given archdiocese or diocese; most of the magazines are the "semiofficial" organs of religious orders or Catholic organizations. Within both groups are publications typed "Catholic by denomination"; within both are others called "Catholic by inspiration." However, the designations are loose and undefined, and if one took a poll on the function of publications in the various classifications, one would receive almost as many answers as persons queried. Even within categories there would be no common agreement. The inevitable consequence of lack of definition is not only a confusion of purposes and objectives,

[37] *Free Speech in the Church* (New York: Sheed and Ward, 1959).
[38] *Ibid.,* p. 26.

but a variety of hybrid editors who as recently as the 1962 Catholic Press Association convention were debating what the Catholic press should be talking about. The convention debate dramatized how badly the Catholic press stands in need of a clearer enunciation of what it is and how it should go about its job— details which should have been settled decades ago.

Happily for those interested, the answer to many of these perplexities is not hard to find; in fact it has been lying around for a quarter-century as an appendix to an undusted book by Jacques Maritain, *True Humanism*.[39] The Maritain theory of publication is one that promises consistency and focus for the Catholic press, while at the same time it widens the avenues for editorial pronouncement and public expression by eliminating the major bogey in the way of "involvement." This is the bogey which leaves the Church press the choice between withdrawal and selected involvement, since the Catholic press as it is presently conceived seems to engage the responsibility of the Church as an institution.

Professor Maritain's theory is embedded in the careful distinction between action in the spiritual order and action in the temporal order, between what belongs to religion and what to the sociotemporal; it is a distinction, to use M. Maritain's words, bound up in the understanding that "to speak as a Catholic having a certain temporal position and to speak in the name of Catholicism are two very different things."[40] One engages oneself; the other the Church. The distinction is not always easily made, and no one is under the illusion that it could be easily translated to Catholic journalism. But it is possible and would seem to be urgent if the Catholic press proposes to serve the City of Man in the measure that it seeks to serve the City of God.

The Maritain theory envisions a "temporal" Catholic press— periodicals which "draw their inspiration in the most courageous and intrepid manner from Christian wisdom" but which "in-

---

[39] Jacques Maritain, *True Humanism* (London, 1938).
[40] *Ibid.*, p. 300.

volve no other initiative than that of the particular persons or groups who have started them."[41] This type of periodical, "this press formally belonging to the temporal plane and Christian by inspiration not denomination, appears to correspond to a vital necessity," Maritain maintains.[42] He sees such a press imparting on the one hand doctrinal information, explanation and commentary on papal encyclicals and acts, and the syntheses of Christian political and social wisdom, and on the other accurate and objective information on all aspects of temporal problems:

> To the extent to which their inspiration is truly and integrally Christian, they witness to the Gospel and serve in an effective way in the penetration of the world and men's lives by Christianity. But the proper aim they set before themselves is not the apostolate; it is the accomplishment of a temporal work, the service of a secular truth, the assuring of an earthly good.[43]

A "temporal" Catholic press could be the occupation of clerics or laity, working either singly or as a mixed team. However, the most advantageous arrangement would seem to be the building of such a press around the laity, since clerics by the very nature of their office involve the Church as an institution in the minds of that vast audience, Catholic as well as non-Catholic, unwilling or unable to make the careful distinctions between official pronouncement of an establishment, and unofficial opinion of members of the establishment.

The case of *America*, a national Catholic review whose temporality is unmistakable, is a study in this difficulty. *America* proclaims weekly in its masthead that it is "published by Jesuits of the United States and Canada." In what it characterized not so long ago as "a kind of self-examination," *America* stressed that the masthead "pointedly does not say that our journal issues from

---

[41] *Ibid.*, p. 303.
[42] *Ibid.*, p. 304.
[43] *Ibid.*, p. 303.

'the Jesuits of the United States and Canada'"; America noted further that in its postal indicia it is described as edited and published by "a group of Jesuit Fathers."[44]

Yet, despite the qualifications, and the clear and repeated statement that the opinions expressed are merely those of the Jesuit priests listed on the masthead, when controversial issues crop up (as they do regularly in America) there is a frequent confusion, arising from the affiliation of its editors, concerning for whom America is speaking—itself, the Catholic Church in America, the Jesuit Order, or, by wildest deduction, the Archdiocese of New York (presumably, since the magazine is published within New York's ecclesiastical geography). There is seldom this confusion when the temporal publication is lay edited and inspired. And this is the key to the Maritain logic. To achieve maximum effectiveness, a "temporal" Catholic press almost of necessity should be a lay responsibility, at least on the editorial level.

A "temporal," lay-edited press is not unknown in America, but examples are so few as to make it a curiosity. One thinks offhand of The Commonweal, Jubilee, The Critic, Catholic Worker, Cross Currents, and, more recently, Ramparts. Of course there are others, but the point is, they are not many. This is greatly to be regretted, for those lay Catholic publications which have elected to perform within the "temporal" orbit have invariably proved fresh and exciting, if not always durable and lucrative. In addition, they have provided a substantial witness, although oftentimes the latter has gone unacknowledged and unappreciated. One wonders, for instance, if due recognition and full thanks were ever extended to Work, the social action tabloid published out of Chicago, or Integrity, the provocative religion-and-life magazine of the late Ed Willock and co-worker Carol Jackson Robinson. In their day, Work and Integrity filled voids ignored by the general Catholic press; however, both publications passed from the scene quietly and unmourned—though the memory of Work lingers in New City (Chicago), a "temporal" magazine

[44] February 10, 1962, pp. 619, 620.

described by its editors as "a Christian response to man in metropolis."[45]

The "temporal" publication which in all respects demonstrates the practicality of the Maritain theory is *The Commonweal,* a weekly review which since 1924 has faced squarely the religious, political, social, and cultural issues confronting the American Catholic, and has done so with an intelligence and conviction that have gained for it a prestige few others in the Catholic press have ever known even briefly. As often as not, *The Commonweal's* voice has been a lonesome one, whether the issue under discussion was Father Coughlin, General Franco, or the expectations of the layman in terms of the Second Vatican Council. But its witness has been important, and its minority viewpoints have survived amazingly well the tests of history.

The lesson of *The Commonweal,* however, is less its record of achievement, and less even the fact that beginning with its founding editor, Michael Williams, it has attracted to its staff laymen of the calibre of George Shuster, Edward Skillin, John Cogley, and James O'Gara—though there is a causality between these particulars and the magazine's "temporal" character well worth meditating. The lesson of *The Commonweal,* rather, is in the witness which can be carried into the temporal order by a publication making no claim to be official or to speak for the Church, and whose editors possess competence, direct responsibility, and the inspiration of Catholic conscience.

Unfortunately, publications assuming such a role can look for neither popularity nor profit. *The Commonweal* has been ducking brickbats most of its life, and its circulation and advertising revenues have always been meager. In 1951, Msgr. George G. Higgins was appealing in his syndicated column for 2,500 new subscribers to *The Commonweal* so that it could "stay in existence for another calendar year,"[46] and in 1962 the magazine was still leaning on the generosity of charter and sustaining members

45 Vol. I, No. 1 (1962), 3.

46 "The Yardstick" column, *Catholic Free Press* (Worcester, Mass.), December 14, 1951, p. 28.

of what is known as Commonweal Associates to help balance the books.[47] The reading public, clerical and lay, remains apathetic. The 1962–63 edition of the *Catholic Press Directory* lists the circulation of *The Commonweal* an anemic 22,068; the figure for *Columbia*, the Knights of Columbus monthly, is 1,076,031, and for the unoffending *Catholic Digest*, 676,665.

It is no one's contention—and certainly not Maritain's—that the Catholic press should be entirely a "temporal" press; the "spiritual" or specifically Catholic publication will always have its place. So will the specialist publications, which serve specific areas of scholarship and cater to particular audiences—magazines such as *Worship* in the liturgical field, *Catholic Biblical Quarterly, Catholic Charities Review, Theology Digest, Catholic Historical Review, Social Order,* and such important university-sponsored journals as Fordham's *Thought* and Notre Dame's *Review of Politics.* Publications such as these have important functions to perform, despite understandably limited circulation potentials. They might be typical of nothing but themselves, yet in given fields of study and apostolic activity, specialized publications are in a position to exert positive and constructive influence, and regularly do so. To deprive them of their voice, or cause their voice to be repitched, would in many, many cases be a disservice to religion and erudition.

In the broader field of the popular press, however, if the Catholic press is seriously interested in penetrating the temporal order and exploiting the advantages which lie in the direction of freer speech and broader witness, then it must explore the Maritain formula for "temporal" publication. At the moment the Catholic press waivers indecisively. Primarily it conducts itself as a spiritual or denominational press, but still it does not renounce its right to occasional "temporal" or secular pronouncement. The consequence is exactly as predicted by Maritain: (1) "temporal" judgments are often weak and indecisive; (2) the reader, "led to believe that he is being supplied with all the necessary means of

[47] *The Commonweal,* May 4, 1962.

judging and of directing his own conduct with regard to these things,"[48] frequently slips into error and disenchantment.

If the Maritain formula is to be explored, the time could hardly be more opportune than the present. American Catholics of to-day are a more mature and sophisticated body whose advance from the elementary Christian Doctrine mentality has yet to be taken fully into account. They are much better educated than before, but so often they are treated as the credulous believers of yesterday, who should be satisfied with the pat answer and be willing to entrench themselves behind the united front.

A focused Catholic press, functioning less on the denominational plane and more in the "temporal" order, would have the double advantage of doing away with current attitudes of spiritual adolescence and, in the process, making itself and its readers more relevant. One becomes enthusiastic about this prospect when he senses that reorientation would not necessarily involve reorganization. In other words, the Catholic press could continue to exist in its present form; direction and emphasis alone would need to be changed.

If a serious approach were ever made to "temporal" publication in line with the Maritain formula, the starting point would have to be the editorial page, if only because that is where opinion and policy originate, and where the seeds of public opinion are sown. But this is much more easily said than done. The editorial page philosophies of the Catholic press are multiple and they offer a clue to the complexity of what might otherwise seem an ordinary problem.

There are some publications which carry no editorials, perhaps with the thought that this guarantees impartiality; there are publications in which the editorials are signed or initialed so that there will be no mistaking whose opinion is being aired; there are publications which carry carefully worded disclaimers or codicils (the Indianapolis *Criterion* runs above its editorials this notation: "The opinions expressed in these editorial columns represent a Catholic viewpoint—not necessarily THE Catholic view-

[48] Maritain, *op. cit.*, p. 300.

point. They are efforts of the editors to serve public opinion within the Church and within the Nation"). Finally, there are journals which publish their editorials unsigned, uninitialed, and unfettered by qualifications, relying on their readers to understand that the only "official" material in their newspaper or magazine is specifically so marked.

There is something to be said for all these procedures (or all except the first), but the last one seems to contain in fullest measure the potentialities for arriving at a "temporal" formula which protects the Church, gives status to the publication, affords intellectual incentive (and protection) to the editors, provides for the thinking Catholic, and increases the impact capabilities of publication. This last procedure demands that other Catholics realize that no Catholic editor is bound to be a parrot; that he is free to editorialize in the knowledge that he is committing no one and nothing beyond himself and his paper; that to so editorialize is not an intrusion on the authority of the Church; that the editor may be right or (heaven forbid!) wrong; and, most important, that he is liable to refutation and correction. The reader-intelligence capable of grasping such a working arrangement is there; it merely awaits the challenge. If and when it comes, look for numerous problems to evaporate, including those of editorial jurisdiction and continuity of editorial conviction.

A "temporal" publication policy would require of editors— apart from the usual gifts of competence, tact, integrity, and charity—what Pius XII called "a profound love and unalterable respect for the divine order which embraces and pervades every aspect of life."[49] By the same token it would impose on clerical supervisors or superiors a new but not impossible tolerance and dispassion.

The policy would not be implemented easily, for it is predicated on the ability of both layman and cleric to distinguish between opinion and pronouncement, counsel and command, and at the same time it asks a magnanimity from those who have the power to restrict published expression to coincide with

[49] *The Pope Speaks*, ed. Michael Chinigo, p. 357.

their own credo. But difficult as all this may be of reconciliation, if only because human natures and long-standing attitudes have to be considered, it seems the direction in which sights must be trained if the Catholic press in America and Catholic press journalists are to become the force everyone agrees they should be but as yet are not. It also seems the answer to attracting to the general Catholic press proportionately larger numbers of lay journalists of the calibre the "temporal" Catholic press has proved it can attract.

Scholarship funds, working conditions, annuity plans, and apostolic motivation will be of limited inducement to aspiring Catholic journalists if the impact potential of the Catholic press is impaired by confusion of function, and if the talents of the journalist are subjected to the caprices of the ordained. The Maritain formula would seem a reasonable basis for at least a partial solution to most of our problems.

A giant step in the direction of the Maritain formula, and toward the solution of the problems which crop up in the paths of ecclesiastical authority and freedom of the Catholic press, was suggested by Msgr. John Tracy Ellis at the 1962 eastern regional convention of the Catholic Press Association.

· Conceding (a) "that bishops are not free—even if they should so desire—to permit in their dioceses publications bearing a Catholic name to speak and to act as though they had no responsibility to the local ecclesiastical authority," and recognizing (b) that the editor and his staff should be allowed "every possible leeway in the exercise of their professional tasks," Msgr. Ellis suggested a revival of the once fairly widespread practice throughout the Church in America of setting aside in the publication one official page for the local bishop. The understanding would be that what appeared on that page was policy; what appeared elsewhere in the publication would have no formal sanction, other than that derived from the competence of the writer and/or publication. Declared Msgr. Ellis: "There, it seems to me, lies the remedy for the 'official' Catholic newspapers that must reconcile two things, that, superficially speaking, seem to be irreconcilable; that is, the bishop's moral obligation to exercise ecclesiastical censorship and supervision, and the freedom of the press that is essential if journalists are to do their job."[50]

If the precedent of what was fairly widespread in yesterday's America is not considered applicable to today's scene, where, unlike yesterday, the vast majority of Catholic publications are owned by the Church, note might be taken of the character of Vatican City's newspaper, *L'Osservatore Romano. Osservatore*—which significantly is lay-edited—customarily carries on its front page the official Vatican press releases. But these have no official status unless they are so marked in each individual case. For, despite the common impression in America, *L'Osservatore Romano* is not an official Vatican organ. The official Vatican publication is *Acta Apostolicae Sedis,* a periodical published in the language of the Church, Latin (*Osservatore* appears in Italian). As *L'Osservatore Romano's* editor of almost forty years, Count Giuseppe Dalla Torre commented before his retirement in 1960: "*Osservatore* is a Catholic newspaper in which the Holy See publishes its official bulletins. Nothing else."[51]

Thus is the Vatican City newspaper enabled to function freely and without involving the papacy or the reigning Pontiff; thus might also the "official" Catholic press in the United States operate—freely and without involving Church, ecclesiastical authority, diocese, or religious order.

THE CATHOLIC PRESS— THE PROBLEM, THE CHALLENGES

In the matter of prerogatives and privileges, as well as on the question of a more extensive "temporal" Catholic press, the lay journalist has not been particularly articulate—which in view of one indispensable consideration is exceedingly discreet. Although

[50] Nov. 8, 1962, in Baltimore, Md. Quotations are taken from text processed by N.C.W.C. News Service, Nov. 12, 1962.

[51] Religious News Service story, as appearing in the *Pittsburgh Catholic,* July 20, 1961.

there is no argument about the professional and technical skills of the lay Catholic journalist, he has proved short on that talent which in the final analysis is the crucial test of his total competence as a worker in religious journalism, and without which not only is he precluded from pressing his personal claims but the Catholic press itself is also shut off from far-reaching and resourceful "temporal" publication.

The missing quality referred to is theological sensitivity—the ability to grasp the theological implications of the world's news and to impart to the understanding of these events, and, in some cases at least, to their evolution, the mind of the Church. On obvious moral levels the layman is competent enough, but in exploring intricate and subtle depths, and bringing to these wise, knowledgeable theological interpretations, there he has shown himself weak.

Some may claim that, given its audience, it is less than imperative for the Catholic press to be steeped in the refinements of theology. This is no argument, however, but merely a somewhat contemptuous denigration of the reader of the Catholic press. Even if it were valid, it would not justify theological superficiality. The Catholic press cannot scale itself to the theological impoverishment of its average reader, any more than it can be indifferent to the hungers of its intellectually and theologically elite. In point of fact, the task is twofold: to elevate the former, while at the same time stimulating the latter.

That a theologically sensitive Catholic press is possible and desirable, even when the broadest readership is being addressed, is evident from the performance of the Boston *Pilot* and the Indianapolis *Criterion*, first-class diocesan newspapers blessed with editors who combine in superb degree the talents of the professional journalist and the relevant theologian. That the editors of both papers happen to be priests (Msgr. Francis J. Lally in the case of *The Pilot*, and Father Raymond T. Bosler at the *Criterion*) does not make the ideal of a theologically perceptive lay-edited Catholic publication any less achievable. Theology is not something that belongs exclusively to the seminary, nor is it the preserve of the ordained; it should be part of the thought and action of any intelligent Catholic, and certainly of the Catholic who is professionally employed as a Catholic and is dealing in the realm of thought and ideas. Very likely much of the problem would be solved if theology enjoyed on the Catholic campus the role claimed for it in commencement oratory. Unfortunately it does not, although currently there are moves in some collegiate circles to correct the situation.

No one contends that the Catholic lay journalist needs the theological erudition of a professor or the total competence of a specialist. But he must have the acquaintance of a scholar if he hopes to move the Catholic press from the static position in which his lack has immobilized it.

Such reasoning was advanced by this writer in an article published earlier in *America*.[52] It excited reactions from several quarters that were quite critical (wouldn't it be simpler to make journalists out of theologians, argued one respondent). Nevertheless it is a rationale in support of which impressive corroborating witness can be called. The distinguished Jesuit editor and author, Father John La Farge, for one, has remarked that "Catholic journalists would be greatly helped by solid theological knowledge," and he views as "particularly urgent . . . the development of the moral theology of the present economic world —ownership and distribution, society and its obligations, as well as those of management and labor."[53] Father Albert J. Nevins, M.M., editor of *Maryknoll*, for another, while president of the Catholic Press Association noted a lack of theological depth among "some" laymen of the Catholic press and commented that, as those editors who come from religious life must acquire technical and sociological training, so "lay editors should be prepared to undertake the study of theology."[54] Bishop John Wright of Pittsburgh has spoken even more forcefully on the subject, at-

52 "What's Missing in the Catholic Press?" February 4, 1961.
53 *The Pilot* (Boston), May 13, 1961, p. 10.
54 "The Catholic Editor: Littérateur or Organizational Man," *Catholic Press Annual 1962*, pp. 4 ff.

tributing to the laity generally a "frightening superficiality of the knowledge of theology."[55] He sees this condition existing throughout most of Christendom, "but especially in our land." Finally, the very existence at the University of San Francisco of an Institute of Lay Theology for adult Catholics who wish to adapt their lives and careers to the service of the Church is evidence that a lay knowledge of theology is both urgent and missing.

In our *America* article we offered recommendations for coping with this problem. We called for renewed emphasis on theological studies in Catholic colleges and universities so that young men and women would be graduated with a keener theological awareness of their political, economic, and social commitments. This we envisioned providing, if not a truly theologically oriented laity, one that was at least theologically disposed. For those already in the workaday world, and with particular reference to lay Catholic journalists, we urged a systematized, intense series of theology seminars geared to matters of moment, which would refine the philosophy of the lay editors and deepen their theological discernments. The proposal made great sense to us, and one official of a Catholic university thought it sufficiently worth while to offer "to co-operate to the fullest extent in any undertaking of this kind" and suggested that the Catholic Press Association appoint a committee to study the matter.[56] But nothing has happened; for the foreseeable future, the Catholic press will have to struggle along with only a handful of journalists (and only a few of them laymen) who possess the theological formation which should belong to all almost without exception.

If the Catholic press can be said to have one overriding problem, one problem which must be eliminated before talk about the potential of the Catholic press can escape the realm of the academic, it is this problem of theologically inept journalists. Correc-

[55] *Pittsburgh Catholic*, June 28, 1962, p. 1.

[56] William K. Trivett, S.J., chairman of the Department of Communication Arts, Fordham University, in a letter to the editor, *America*, February 25, 1961.

tion of this situation is vital both for the impact of the Catholic press on its readership, and on an age which, as others have pointed out, is increasingly disposed to listen to the informed layman, often in preference to the ordained minister of God.

Should a corps of theology-centered journalists be trained from the laity, and should the Catholic press move then to adopt a formula for "temporal" publication (again, the second is predicated on the first), we could look for multiple changes from the press as it presently exists. The most immediate change, it can safely be predicted, is that in facing more toward the world the Catholic press would turn its back on much of its present clericalism and parochialism—that fixation with men of the cloth and preoccupation with family affairs which advertise to those outside the household that the Catholic press is a house organ written by, for, and about Catholics. The symptoms of the latter are manifold: the inordinate number of pictures of the Ordinary (it is not unusual in some diocesan newspapers to see as many as a half-dozen pictures of the bishop in a single issue); the inevitable presence of Father or Sister in the parish committee picture (what surer way to dull lay initiative?); the Catholic-angle approach to secular affairs; and the tribal interpretations placed on events and incidents of disparate genera. There might have been a time when it was worth noting that Anthony Celebrezze was the seventeenth Catholic to be appointed to a Cabinet post; it is doubtful if there ever was a day when the severity of an Atlantic hurricane could be gauged by the damage done an Order's beach home, or the force of a midwestern tornado be judged by the injuries caused Catholics. Yet much of the Catholic press has shown a marked proclivity for approaches like these.

There may be less of this sectarianism in the Catholic press now than there once was, but a considerable gap remains to be bridged before the Catholic press arrives at the notion implicit in the life and the thought of Pius XII, that nothing is foreign to the Church save only sin and error, and the implications in John XXIII's counsel to the Catholic Union of the Italian Press: that the Catholic journalist must be prepared "to defend and help defend truth, justice, honesty, even before religion and the Gospel."[57] A synthesis of these ideas is urgent if the Catholic press hopes to become a medium whose thoughts on temporal affairs will be anxiously solicited, instead of indifferently awaited and cynically discounted.

It may seem paradoxical to cite a Spanish bishop in discussing the Catholic press in America. Nevertheless, the advice of Bishop Pedro Cantero of Huelva to the School of Journalism of the Church, Madrid, is worth tne attention of American Catholic publishers and editors:

> The Catholic press must differ from the secular press solely by its spirit and its conception. We have no right to oblige a Catholic paper, both by its contents and its presentation, to look like a pious almanac . . . The Catholic paper must take its place in the perspective of everyday life, be an instrument in the publication of daily news, and reflect the lives of men and peoples, their thoughts, their questions, their preoccupations and their hopes. A paper that does not take its news from passing events and gives no answer to the questions of the hour, is a paper doomed to disappear.[58]

In this perspective, the Catholic press in America—whether the publication be a diocesan newspaper or a specialized journal such as the *Catholic Lawyer*—should be concerned in maximum degree with the wide world and the broad common good, as distinct from the precincts of the Church and the good circumscribed by Catholic interests and partisanships. This would in no way remove the Catholic press from the intrinsic life of the Church—its societies, its good works, its evangelistic mission— nor would it diminish its role as educator and defender of the faith. If anything, the opposite would be the case, and an indebtedness would grow from the witness which the Catholic

[57] *Bulletin International,* Union Internationale de la Presse Catholique (Paris), January–February, 1961, p. 4.
[58] *Ibid.,* p. 7.

press would be carrying into fields which, though doctrinally neutral, have an appeal to the humanitarianism of Catholics both as Christians and as citizens, with all that both words imply.

One thinks of public housing, urban renewal, the migrant worker, the senior citizen, fair employment and housing practices, depressed work areas, crime commissions, slum clearance, government surplus food plans, and a host of related topics. If the Catholic press made issues such as these matters of instinctive instead of sporadic interest, there is no calculating the stature it would attain in the "family" as well as in society generally.

A Catholic press with restraints relaxed by "temporal" operation, and with a scope as wide as that suggested (or wider), would likely have the bonus effect of modifying what tend to become monologues on subjects which are delicate by nature (administration, education, family planning, and so forth), and on which there is an absence of really constructive dialogue between Catholics themselves. This would be particularly true where publications provided letter-to-the-editor forums that were free, in *fact* as well as in theory, for the expression of opinion. Clergy-lay channels would be opened up considerably, and contact and understanding would improve on numerous hushed subjects.

Obviously, the Catholic publication which confronts Church and temporal affairs boldly and impartially will be sharply criticized. Readers accustomed to a press of detachment, and anesthetized by the frivolous, tend to regard interior dialogue as a display of disloyalty or even anticlericalism; and concern for the world can easily become interpreted as suspiciously secularist. The writer recalls, in this connection, a letter received at the *Pittsburgh Catholic* after it had stepped into the "temporal" arena. "I'm sick and tired of opening the *Pittsburgh Catholic* and finding nothing to read but Liberal, Conservative, Integration, Urban Renewal, Medical Aid to the Aged, RIDC [Regional Industrial Development Corporation], Fair Housing, etc.," the reader wrote. "A religious paper should at least attempt to make people better and calmer, not get their tempers up. . . . Getting people to heaven is more important than whether a certain section of town is run down, or certain people are not preferred to others, or how the aged should be taken care of."

The temptation is to dismiss such crank complaints impatiently, and to write them off as the expression of the hostile and unenlightened attitudes of status-quo Catholics. But the Catholic press cannot be complacent about this; it bears a measure of accountability for this insensitivity, and hence has a consequent obligation for re-education, so that Catholics like this one might be lifted above their isolation, self-interest, and secular stoicism. The Catholic press must remember that, no matter how well it has served devotional and organizational Catholicism, it has too long neglected areas which should have been of basic Catholic concern.

Turn back just a few years. As Pius XII pleaded for an international consciousness, much of the Catholic press was bogged down in the pro's and con's of domestic communism and the "godlessness" of the United Nations; as important papers and speeches were reduced to innocuous synopses, reams of copy were supplied on wonders of doubtful significance (what reader in the Catholic press is not familiar with the phenomena of new stigmata or a miraculous spring?); as readers were familiarized with the civil services of faraway Vatican City (its jail, railway station, fire department, and so forth), these same services in the locale of publication were left undiscussed, even unmentioned; as generous space was devoted to sports, socials, and dedications, movements of historical import (liturgical, Christian Family, interracial) received perfunctory treatment.

Consequently if the Catholic press has a problem today about a fringe-Catholic readership, it is partially because it, itself, has been a fringe-Catholic press.

It is precisely at this point that challenges crystallize.

The Catholic press first must instill in its readers a keener sense of community, a sense of belonging and caring, from the local to the international levels, and in the ecumenical as well as in any temporal sphere of interest; secondly, it must supply inspiration and motivation to him whom Donald Thorman so accurately types "the emerging layman." Both challenges have civic, political, cultural, intellectual, and religious implications, and the meeting of them depends on a Catholic press of vision, depth, and perception. A Catholic press with strong propensities for crusades on issues in which there are legal complexities, and/or a variety of moral attitudes in the community (for instance, birth control, Sunday sales, censorship), will never produce a readership sensitive to the larger considerations of life in a pluralistic society or capable of making much of a positive contribution to its milieu. Likewise, a Catholic press engrossed in banalities will never be able to fulfill the obligations of thoughtfulness that it has to a Catholic population which may be presumed to be interested more and more in things of the mind, and less and less in sentimentalism and emotionalism.

No one in recent years sensed these challenges or saw the corresponding editorial responsibilities more clearly than did Donald McDonald, who joined the *Catholic Messenger* of Davenport in 1949 as a young World War II veteran, and who pioneered so much of what was to be adopted widely (though nowhere near widely enough) by others of the Catholic press. In a sense, young McDonald was the harbinger of the new breed of Catholic editor; his innovations included documentation, depth reporting, interpretation, serious critiques, and an appreciation of the fine arts theretofore largely unknown in the cultural wasteland that was then the Catholic press. One result of the McDonald perspicacity was that this newspaper, of a relatively obscure Iowa diocese, won a national reading audience as word got around that here, at last, was a paper which considered it its business to rescue from oblivion full texts of addresses delivered before limited audiences on subjects liturgical, social, economic, educational, theological, philosophical; a newspaper so aware of the education in which Catholics stood need that it published, in serial form and with editor's commentary, classical encyclicals of continuing pertinence—"Quadragesimo Anno" (1931), "Mediator Dei" (1947), "Mystici Corporis"

(1943); a paper that gave to literature and the arts the knowledgeable review and evaluation which these merited but were usually denied in the Catholic press.

No one is under the illusion, and least of all Donald McDonald, that a publication stressing temporal and intellectual content will have blanket appeal. However, as Mr. McDonald points out, even though only a minority of the editor's readers will be interested and will profit from this material, it is an important minority, and too long and too often it is a minority which has not found much in the diocesan press that can be helpful. Moreover, it is the minority that influences others—teachers and professors, professional people and college graduates of intellectual vitality, people who should have something to feed on in the general Catholic press without having to search out the half-dozen diocesan newspapers and the half-dozen magazines which offer intellectual stimulation.

Mr. McDonald (whose business now is producing journalists; he is dean of the Marquette University School of Journalism) explains that it has always struck him as curious that more diocesan editors are concerned with supplying sports data, social news, and insipid features—to the person who devours this type of material—than are concerned about catering to the intellectuals in their readership:

What can be more important for a Catholic weekly than providing substantial intellectual fare for the increasingly numerous college and university graduates in its readership? For instance, how can it better use that half-page or page each week that should be devoted to "documentation"—more pictures of brides or adolescent basketball players? Or the local Ordinary receiving the latest in an endless series of checks?

The editor who gives, say, a half-page a week to "documentation" should be prepared for the criticism that will come from the anti-intellectuals that "the paper is too heavy for the ordinary reader." The assumption beneath this criticism is always that "the whole paper" is devoted to documentation. The assumption, obviously, is false, but it exists.[59]

Actually, if criticism is to be leveled (and this is an expression of regret rather than criticism), it is that publications of the strong intellectual purposes of the Davenport *Messenger* (of the McDonald and, equally, the John Leo periods) are not more common, and especially that they do not exist in certain metropolitan areas or in sees within whose geography there exist prominent centers of learning and of state, national, and world government.

It is an unhappy fact that in so many key cities where the Catholic press stands to exert positive and constructive influence, there it is impotent and ineffectual. This is a serious problem all by itself; fortunately, it is also a problem which is beginning to trouble many.

It is hardly necessary to accept the conclusions of this essay in order to concede that the Catholic press could be improved and thereby offer greater service to God, Church, and Nation. Who would be so naive as to argue that we have achieved the ideal in this area of publishing? We need, accordingly, to face up to what Msgr. John Tracy Ellis calls the "difficult and exacting task of self-scrutiny, of analyzing and criticizing ourselves among ourselves"[60]—in this instance the Catholic press. This does not promise to be a very pleasant project, because of what Msgr. Ellis labels the "super-sensitiveness"[61] of the Catholic press, not only to criticism from without, but also to criticism within and (as anyone associated any length of time with the Catholic press might add) to criticism of itself. Resistance is inevitable and, for that matter, understandable. To subject the

[59] Donald McDonald to author, March 15, 1962.

[60] Msgr. Ellis at the June, 1960 symposium on "The Present Position of Catholicism in America," held at Rosary College, River Forest, Illinois, under sponsorship of the Thomas More Association and the Rosary College Department of Library Science.

[61] Address to the Eastern regional convention of the Catholic Press Association, November 8, 1962.

Catholic press to hard, honest reappraisal would undoubtedly injure, perhaps mortally, some publications. But the end result would be a strengthening, not a weakening, of the whole body.

The Catholic press has entered upon new and trying times. The challenges that must be met also indicate opportunities for the development of a truly vital religious press.

For one thing, the decline in the number of secular magazines and daily newspapers (with a corresponding decline in editorial voices and reportorial eyes) highlights both the need and the opportunity to assume involvements which too often have been ignored. It now appears likely that Catholic journals will survive the forces of merger and absorption that are constantly cutting into the general press. Even if economic pressure should cause a pruning of the Catholic press, however, the results need not be harmful. The mission of the Catholic press might be more effectively realized if there were fewer journals, and if those with a professionally serious and well-defined function had less competition from house organs and fund-raising publications.

Secondly, the existence of larger numbers of people—and even, seemingly, of whole nations—who are ignorant, indifferent, suspicious, or hostile in regard to religion, only underlines the need for excellence in a press whose very reason for existence is to bear witness to spiritual values and to seek their application in the world and in the affairs of men.

The challenge to the American Catholic press thus takes on prophetic dimensions quite different from any it has previously known. We must look out beyond our parish boundaries and see our problems in more than regional or even national terms. Nor can we reduce the challenge to the threat of international communism, despite its formidable ideological and military presence. We might, in fact, discover that a large part of the antireligious critique can have a positive value by freeing us of many inadequate conceptions in which we tend to imprison the values we wish to serve.

The Catholic press must make increasingly clear that what is at stake is not sectarian advantage, but the preservation of the deepest insights of this civilization that we fumblingly and not quite accurately refer to as Western and Judaeo-Christian. The term "Catholic" will be seen in its full meaning if, as mankind struggles to recapture a lost unity, we join wholeheartedly in the fight, reminding the world that there is a God, and that the creature called "man" exists in His image and for this reason is entitled to dignity and respect.

In pursuing such objectives, the Catholic press is fortunate in being able to draw on many bright examples in the life of Pope John XXIII. We can draw the needed lessons, from his elimination of slurring references to Jews from the official prayers of the Church; from his promulgation of "Mater et Magistra," the encyclical which is the blueprint for co-operative effort in the material redemption of man; from the solicitude and cordiality which were the hallmarks of his pontificate, and which were especially manifest in the courtesy visits with spokesmen for non-Catholic bodies; from his calling of the whole Church into council and his invitations to Vatican II of non-Catholic delegate-observers; and from "Pacem in Terris," Pope John's masterful guide for peace in an orderly world, significantly addressed to "all men of good will."

So much of the fear and distrust that accumulated over the centuries was dispelled by that gentle and beloved Pope. In correlation, there has developed an air of understanding, mutual trust, and, yes, fraternal love in which men of good will of all creeds can come together for the exchange of ideas and discussion about their hopes, problems, and resolves. This is the spirit in which the Catholic press must now get to work. It is the spirit, the mood of "aggiornamento," in which Pope Paul VI appears to have launched his pontificate.

3 The Jewish Press:

A QUADRILINGUAL PHENOMENON

DAVID WOLF SILVERMAN

IN APPROACHING such a varied phenomenon as the press of American Jewry, we must first bear in mind that until the end of the First World War the American Jewish press was quadrilingual and is today trilingual. A measure of linguistic competence in German, Yiddish, Hebrew, and English is a prerequisite for understanding its history, function, and current problems. Part of the fascination of the tumultuous history of this press is the battle concerning the legitimacy of the languages in which it appeared. For the first three decades of the twentieth century, the index to cultural sophistication among Jews was decisive mastery of English prose. As part of the process of Americanizing the Jewish immigrant, the Yiddish press published lessons in English. Fluency in the use of English was regarded as the key to social and personal success. As noted below, the rise of an American-Jewish, in contradistinction to a Yiddish and Hebrew, press was the direct outcome of the success of the latter in accommodating the economically aspiring and socially mobile immigrant to his new milieu. But the true battle of legitimacy among languages took place between the proponents of Yiddish as the characteristic national speech of the Jews and the brave band of Hebraists who always constituted the numerical minority. Although waged in bitterness, the battle was won not on these shores but in Israel, where the adoption of Hebrew as the official language of the state made Yiddish, once the *lingua franca* of the Jewish masses, a linguistic backwater.

Even more paradoxical is the invocation of the adjective "religious" as applied to the American Jewish press. There does exist a "denominational press"—one which variously expresses the viewpoints and organizational needs of Conservative, Reform, and Orthodox Judaism. Without exception, this consists of monthlies, quarterlies, and annuals which are either house organs or scholarly journals. The fact is that the dialectical relationship of Judaism and the Jews (the one being inconceivable without the other, while both are ultimately connected with mankind) did not easily produce the amalgam of a "religious press." In its origin and even at the height of its influence, a good part of the American Jewish press was avowedly secular. This secular quality, however, did not possess the strident anticlerical overtones of a press opposed to religion and religious institutions. Its literary medium (Yiddish and Hebrew), its calendar, and its characteristic topics were all suffused by the Jewish religious tradition. Yiddish contains a large number of loan words from biblical Hebrew, while modern Hebrew is directly rooted in the tongue of the prophets and sages of Israel. It is thus difficult, if not impossible, to escape religion in discussing the Jewish press. I shall deliberately situate the "denominational press" within the more general rubric of the Jewish press, for the two differ as to their participation in "religion" only in terms of degree and organizational sponsorship. Gerhard Lenski's recent study seems to offer confirmation of this approach; he found that although "the ties binding individual Jews to their religious association have been weakened in modern times, the ties of communalism remain strong."[1] It must be remembered, too, that in Judaism this communalism has religious significance, since it provides the first step in the creation of a "holy community."

[1] *The Religious Factor* (New York: Doubleday/Anchor Books, 1962), p. 37.

THE HISTORICAL
BACKGROUND

It was not an accident that the first Jewish periodical appeared in the Judaeo-Spanish dialect of Ladino in the city of Amsterdam. The year was 1678 and the paper was named *Gazeta de Amsterdam*. Amsterdam was also the home of the second Jewish periodical; but this venture appeared in the Judaeo-German dialect called Yiddish and was named the *Dienstagishi und Freitagishi Courantin*—the "Tuesday and Friday Courant." The life of both papers was very brief. The *Courant*, the longer-lived of the two, remained in existence for only sixteen months.

Two things are significant about these periodicals. The Jewish press arose in a relatively liberal and bustling commercial environment—in this case the city of Amsterdam. In both instances, the titles of the papers gave no indication of their Jewish orientation or content; titles then in current use, such as "gazette" or "courant," became standard. Three hundred years later, in 1916, when the Yiddish newspaper was to reach the peak of its circulation (762,910), the same two factors would apply with equal relevance.

From both the historical and theological viewpoint, the development of a daily or monthly press in premodern times would have been an anachronism. Even as late as 1900, the number of Jewish publishers in Europe was quite small, and their presses were mostly devoted to the production of prayer books, rabbinic legal novellae, and religious reading for women.[2] The infinite yet unbounded world of the religious Jew could not admit in principle the urgency of the everyday as reported by a newspaper. The Jew marked time by the passage of Sabbaths and feast days on the religious calendar. The world, as backdrop for secular advancement, for activities unrelated to the religious quest and

[2] Jacob Reich, "Di yiddishe zeitungen un di englishe—ah fargleich," supplement to the 65th anniversary edition of the *Jewish Daily Forward*, December 30, 1962, p. 3.

task, was a reality grudgingly admitted to Jewish consciousness. Time itself was split between the six workdays and the Sabbath toward which they pointed and for which they existed. It was inadmissible that the latter could be dominated by the former, or even that they could coexist as equal partners in the life of man. For Judaism, the Sabbath is a foretaste of the perfect world to come, in which every weekday will be a Sabbath.

From the point of view of their Christian neighbors, the Jews formed a society on the margin; an association of religious dissenters who could be tolerated only as a "pariah people," demonstrating by their collective existence the validity of Christian truth. To Jewish eyes, their precarious collective existence was that of a kingdom in exile—a spiritual kingdom, awaiting the return of ancient glory, restoration to its land, and redemption of all mankind. This sense of shared destiny is not fertile ground for the production of periodicals. Being omnipresent, this compact vision did not have to be fostered by more than concentration upon the holy texts. This lost world, where study of the Torah (the "Teaching": the translation "Law" traduces the religious weight of the word) promoted both compassion and community, is elegiacally evoked in this account by Abraham Joshua Heschel:

A blazing passion permeated all intellectual activities. It is an untold, perhaps incommunicable story of how mind and heart could merge into one. Immersed in complicated legal discussions, they could at the same time feel the anguish of the Divine Presence that abides in exile . . . In endeavoring to unravel some perplexity raised by a seventeenth century commentary on the Talmud, they were able in the same breath to throb with sympathy for Israel and all afflicted people. Study was a technique for sublimating feeling into thought, for transposing dreams into syllogisms, for expressing grief in difficult theoretical formulations, and joy by finding a solution to a difficult passage in Maimonides. Tension of the soul found an outlet in contriving clever, almost insolvable riddles. In inventing new logical devices to explain the Word of God, they thrilled with yearning after the Holy. To contrive an answer to gnawing doubts was the highest joy. Indeed, there was a whole world of subdued gaiety and sober frolic in the playful subtleties of their pilpul. Their conscious aim, of course, was not to indulge in self-expression—they were far from being intent upon exploiting the Torah—but humbly to partake of spiritual beauty. Carried away by the mellow, melting chant of Talmud-reading, one's mind soared high in the pure realm of thought, away from this world of facts and worries, away from the boundaries of the here and now, to a region where the Divine Presence listens to what Jews create in the study of His Word.[3]

In such a world, history does not exist. The yesterday of the Bible, the today of the exile were merely preludes to the redemption of tomorrow. The drastic shift in religious values caused by the shattering of this proto-religious community can be seen in the contrasting statement of a contemporary Jewish publicist: "The English-Jewish press *is the spiritual guardian of Judaism in America.*" We shall examine the warrant of his claim below. What is important to note is that the latter-day claim can be made only in a world radically different from the theocentric world of premodern Jewry.

The creation and development of a Jewish press, first in Europe and later in the United States, depended upon the twin forces of Emancipation and *Enlightenment,* which first intruded upon and then shattered the religious world of medieval Jewry.

"To the Jews as a nation, we owe nothing; to the Jews as human beings, everything." In delivering this epigram before the French National Assembly on December 23, 1791, Clermont-Tonnerre neatly set the program and problem of Jewish emancipation. No longer could Jews claim to be a separate people, a spiritual kingdom of priests whose legal privileges and disabilities

[3] *The Earth is the Lord's: The Inner World of the Jew in East Europe* (New York: Abelard-Schuman Limited, 1950), pp. 49–51.

were weighed and balanced by the Church. Now Jews had to merge their corporate nature into the collectivity of their host-nation. Liberty, equality, and fraternity had to be extended to the Jews—otherwise the overthrow of *l'ancien regime* would remain incomplete. The award of equal rights, first offered by the Assembly and then zealously taken up by the Jews themselves, became the focus of the political problem of Jewish emancipation. The end of their political disabilities, however, was conditional upon Jewish repudiation of their corporate religious nature and historic structure. They had to become nationals of the countries in which they resided. Jewish courts of law would now disappear, for they were stripped of status and sanction. Jews were to become Frenchmen or Germans or Italians of "the Mosaic persuasion." For Jews, this conversion of Judaism into a religious confession devoid of influence upon the organized social structure is the major revolution of modernity. The problem of political emancipation was but the forerunner of a whole array of dualisms which came to plague the soul and worry the conscience of modern Jewry. Universalism and particularism, humanism and Judaism, freedom and faith became dichotomies, whose resolution usually was effected by dropping or denying the second term in each.

It would, of course, be foolish to ignore the positive side of this revolution. Centuries of closure in the ghetto, of political degradation and economic and social servitude, had prepared an explosion in the latter part of the eighteenth century. The French Revolution was welcomed by great numbers of western European Jews; and when, a half century later, its message was clearly heard by Jews east of the Rhine, it would be received with sympathy. Nevertheless, all modern Jewish social trends derive, in one fashion or another, from the unsolved problem of emancipation. Caught between alienation with its consequent inequality, and nationalization with its corollary, the abandonment of separate status, the Jews opted for the latter.

A fascinating glimpse of the Jewish soul in transition can be gained from looking into the literature of the period of the Enlightenment, when supporters of the *Haskalah* movement became

the first to use periodicals in a deliberate attempt to promulgate
their ideals among the Jewish masses. Until the modern period,
Jews had a sacred literature; secular learning and literature, even
during the Golden Age in Spain, was secondary in seriousness
and ultimacy. The *Maskilim* (literally, "the enlightened") attempted to raise the ideals of the French Revolution and the
German humanists to the position of ultimate values; modern
culture became the norm for sacred culture. Beginning with
Ha-Meassef ("The In-gathering"), a long line of Hebrew and
Yiddish monthlies and weeklies promulgated refinement in man-
ners, morals, and religion. Similarly, German Jewry was responsible for the birth and growth of the *Wissenschaft des Juden-
tums* (the historico-scientific study of Judaism), which sought
to demonstrate, by research into the Jewish past, the eligibility of
Jews to the rights of burghers. Such research was bound to discover the significance of Judaism in the general intellectual and
spiritual context of humanity. Recast as a "spiritual idea" and
armed with equal rights, Judaism and the Jews could become
part of the world. The Jewish world would eventually be absorbed into the European world. "The moral and social equality
of Jews will be the result of the equality of Jewish scientific
research."[4] Scientific research would be the universal solvent for
the problems of mankind; the distinctions between Jew and non-
Jew would be relegated to the dustbins of the past. One of the
founders of Jewish scientific research, Emmanuel Wolff, could
proclaim with messianic fervor, "If ever one bond will embrace
the entire species of man, it will be the bond of scientific knowledge, the bond of pure reason, the bond of truth."[5] This statement is typical of that belated enthusiasm for the Enlightenment
which animated the *Maskilim,* both western and eastern, and
which produced the Jewish press. Within this new medium of
communication two directions could be discerned: outward, to
the general world where the honor of the Jewish community was
at stake; and inward, toward the Jewish community where its

[4] L. Zunz, *Gesammelte Schriften,* Vol. I, p. 59.
[5] *Zeitschrift für die Wissenschaft des Judentuums,* Vol. I (1882), p. 24.

avowed object was to transform it in accordance with the superior standards of the world outside. These two directions, defensive and reconstructive, remain basic to the Jewish press today.

THE YIDDISH PRESS IN THE UNITED STATES

No sector of American Jewish journalism calls up as many nostalgic associations or summarizes an era as neatly as does the Yiddish press. Most of the Jews now resident in the United States are second- or third-generation descendants of Yiddish-speaking immigrants. To their parents or grandparents, the Yiddish press was guide and teacher in regard to the character of the New World. Second only to the public school in impact and influence, the Yiddish press was the most powerful Americanizing agency operative on the Jewish scene. This was proudly acknowledged by the *Daily Forward's* editorial in its 65th anniversary edition:

> *To help the workingman and the Jewish immigrant in this new land were the main reasons for the founding of this paper.* The *Forward* has changed with the times but has never deviated from its original goal: to help improve the living conditions of the workingman and create a better world. . . . No other paper . . . has been of such help *in educating masses of people to a completely new way of life.* The *Forward* reader of the older generation looked on this paper as his *only and most reliable guide* in the new strange world. [Italics added.]

The growth and decline of the Yiddish press tells the story of the arrival of the American Jewish community at bourgeois status. In 1916, when the Jewish population of the United States numbered two-and-one-half to three million, there were ten daily Yiddish newspapers and their combined circulation was 762,910. In the 1960s, with a Jewish population that has almost doubled, there are only two Yiddish daily newspapers left, and their total circulation across the country is less than 140,000.

Although often sensational, crude, and melodramatic, the Yiddish press nevertheless loosed the floodgates of an enormous creative and emotional energy. If Hutchins is right in saying that the function of a newspaper is to teach, the Yiddish newspapers and monthlies fulfilled this function with impressive regularity. The whole range of issues discussed within radical political movements were matters of concern, since these papers were proletarian in origin. Most of the Yiddish dailies at the height of their circulation were allied to definite parties—political or religious, and sometimes both at once—and the cut and thrust of impassioned debate was a constant feature. The art of invective flowered, as newspapers representing socialist and communist tendencies fought for circulation in the years just before and after the Russian revolution.[6]

All was not pedagogy and polemic, however. Jewish wit could be found in abundance in special pages devoted to the subject. In its more mordant stories, Jewish humor served to teach the new immigrant American mores; it was part of the compact and allusive ethos which bound together reader and publicist, and which reflected the intimacy and colloquial character of the Yiddish language itself. Yiddish writers and editors did not feel their readers to be part of an undifferentiated mass. Both partook actively in a living culture, in which whole dimensions of meaning could be communicated by a turn of phrase, or a quotation from the sacred literature. The "insider" quality of this journalism is also evident in the intense partisanship which it generated. Loyalty to one or another of the Yiddish dailies, or to one or more of their many pundits, took on aspects of family allegiance.

With the exception of those papers which had a definite orthodox religious orientation, Jewish religious institutions and personal piety were depicted by the Yiddish press as betrayals of the cosmopolitan ideals of the working class, or at least as irrelevant

[6] J. C. Rich, "The Jewish Labor Movement in the United States," *The Jewish People, Past and Present* (1948), Vol. I; "The Role of the *Jewish Daily Forward* in the Trade Union Movement," *Forward,* May 25, 1947; Mordecai Soltes, *The Yiddish Press, an Americanizing Agency* (1924).

to modern life and to the struggle to improve the conditions of the immigrant. Terms used by European radicals against the Catholic Church were hurled against bearded pietists of New York's Lower East Side; Jewish religion was denounced as "reactionary benightedness and a prop of capitalism." Jewish religion was now replaced by "Jewishness," an amorphous mystical quality compounded of unequal parts of labor solidarity, vast quantities of sentimental *kitsch* with regard to family ties, and memories of an eastern European upbringing. Jewish labor leaders rarely admitted of any real Jewish interests that went beyond proletarian bounds.[7]

According to the most reliable authority, the Yiddish press in the United States began with the lithographed issues of *Di Yiddishe Zeitung* (The Jewish Journal), a weekly edited by J. K. Buchner, which began publication March 1, 1870. It was succeeded in August, 1871 by another weekly, *Di Post*, edited by Henry Bernstein.

Two things are noteworthy with regard to the date and language of these pioneer efforts. The first periodical in Yiddish to achieve any measure of circulation success had appeared in Russia only seven years before, beginning as a supplement to the Hebrew weekly, *Hamelitz* (The Advocate). In addition, although Russia for generations had been the site of the largest Jewish community in the world, it produced no Yiddish daily until 1903, almost two decades after one was started in the United States.

A second feature of interest was the character of the language used. The Yiddish of this American weekly press was heavily Germanic in style and idiom. Although Yiddish had originated in the region of the Rhine between the tenth and twelfth centuries, it became a distinct language in its own right because of accretion from Hebrew, Polish, and Russian. At the beginning, the crudity of the language could be summed up by saying that it consisted of German words transliterated into Hebrew charac-

---

[7] Will Herberg, "The Jewish Labor Movement in the United States," *American Jewish Year Book*, Vol. LIII (1952), 54–55.

ters. Given the crucible of time and circumstance, both the semiotic and syntax of the language underwent considerable change. Because of its hybrid origin, Yiddish became a subject for heated debates in the nineteenth century as to its fitness for literary expression. Its opponents spoke of it sneeringly as a "jargon." Its protagonists could look upon it as a worthy and irreplaceable part of the Jewish national genius, a true "mother tongue" (*mame loshen*), since it alone expressed the soul and essence of the folk.

Prior to 1870, a small weekly and monthly press had catered to the needs, both social and religious, of the German Jews in the United States. With increased German immigration, it began supplementing its English with German editions. A somewhat analogous change took place in the Yiddish weeklies; in the process, the language utilized was so Germanized that it reverted to the Yiddish of four centuries earlier, instead of mirroring the swift colloquial speech of the Yiddish then spoken and written in Europe.

During the 1870s, the Yiddish press served not only as a guide to the New World but as a link with the Old. Buchner's and Bernstein's periodicals constituted the only means of communication between the immigrant and the relatives who still remained "on the other side." An editorial published in the quadrilingual—Yiddish, Hebrew, German, and English—weekly, *The Hebrew News* (April 5, 1871), stated, "Hundreds and thousands of our brothers live here. Those arriving every day speak and understand no other language but the one spoken among our brothers in Russia and Poland. Despite their intelligence and civic spirit, these Jews cannot express their desires in matters of state, for they know no other language. For this reason and because they want to know what is going on in their old home, they need a newspaper in their own language. The publishers therefore plan to issue this paper in a clear and easy Hebrew, a simple Jewish, German, and a lucid English."

The appearance of Yiddish periodicals did not invite universal applause on the part of their chronological precursor, the

English-Jewish press. The first English-Jewish weekly in the United States was *The Asmonean* (*sic!*), which appeared in New York in 1849, edited by Robert Lyons. As early as 1823 a monthly, *The Jew*, was published in New York to help combat the work of Christian missionaries among Jewish immigrants. Other journals, such as *The Occident* and *The Jewish Advocate*, appeared as early as 1843, but their news columns were afterthoughts to their scholarly interests. A later but more influential effort was *The Israelite*, founded in Cincinnati in 1854; its first editor was Isaac Mayer Wise, whose organizational genius and editorial flair were placed in the service of Reform Judaism, which he helped to make the favored denomination of the fast-acculturating German immigrant. Additional English-Jewish weeklies sprang up in San Francisco (*The Jewish Times*, 1855), and New York (*The Jewish Messenger*, 1857, and *The Jewish Record*, 1862).

Such a press could only resent the appearance of Yiddish weeklies, which were considered to be written in the wrong language, for the wrong people, who worshiped the wrong way and pursued the wrong way of life. These extreme judgments can easily be located in the English-Jewish press of the time. *The Jewish Times* declared that *Di Yiddishe Zeitung* was "just as ridiculous as its language"; *The American Israelite* denounced *Di Post* because it felt "that the Yiddish language amuses the masses and makes a mockery of Judaism, whose pure idea is degraded by being clothed in such a language. This country has enough writers of trash and there is no need of this Babel of tongues to render us ridiculous."

Because of the hostility of the English-Jewish press, representing the dominant values of the wealthier and more Americanized German Jews, the Yiddish press increasingly viewed itself as the voice of the Jewish masses. Until the middle of the 1880s, most of the Yiddish press was favorable to an amalgam of religion and enlightenment; socially it leaned toward conservatism. Although some 50,000 European Jews were in the United States by the end of the seventies, the weeklies and monthlies printed in Yiddish had only a limited number of readers and were in continual economic difficulties.

The Yiddish press began to flourish only after the Czarist-sanctioned pogroms of 1881 forced hundreds of thousands of Russian Jews to emigrate to the United States. These new arrivals were conversant with only one language—Yiddish. In 1885 the *Yiddishes Tageblatt* (Jewish Daily News), the first Yiddish daily in the world, was founded by Kasriel Z. Sarasohn. At first the *Tageblatt* affected a heavily Germanized style and its readers consisted mainly of Orthodox Jews, allied with the nascent Zionist movement. It did not appear on the Sabbath or holy days, its editor believing that by its absence on these days it reinforced the religious convictions of its readers![8]

The rising tide of Jewish immigration from Russia and Poland effected a basic change in the style and substance of the Yiddish press. The arrival of capable Yiddish journalists had a positive effect on its readability, since the first concern of these writers was to reach the man in the street with a socio-political message. Propaganda of whatever sort demands ease and fluidity of style. The ponderous Judaeo-German of the 1870s was completely unsuited for this purpose. In the *Vokhnblatt* (Jewish Weekly), Getzel Selikovitch (1863–1926), one of the most popular Yiddish writers, sounded the note of linguistic transformation: "We must speak to the reader in the language he understands best, the language in which lullabies were sung to him, the language in which he mumbled his first words before he was weaned, the language with which he took his first step into the everyday world, the language in which he conducts his daily affairs and in which he has sighed, flattered, mourned, rejoiced and loved." Abraham Cahan, who was to become the editor of the *Jewish Daily Forward*, the largest and most powerful Jewish daily in the

[8] The same policy is still pursued, but with an interesting variation, by the *Tog-Morgen-Zhurnal*, whose religious orientation recalls that of the long defunct *Tageblatt*. The *Morgen-Zhurnal* does not appear officially on the Sabbath, but the *Tog* does, despite the fact that they are one newspaper; this compromise is achieved by simply removing the name *Morgen-Zhurnal* from the masthead on the appropriate days!

world, stressed the difficulties of purifying Yiddish from Germanic and Russian adhesions. "The Yiddish language is composed of words of various origin. It is without rules or grammar. We deem it inadvisable to have in our periodical only one type of Yiddish. Our readers need not be surprised, therefore, that different articles are written in different types of Yiddish. We only believe it important to eliminate all Russian words from our periodical."

More important than the semantic problem was the radical political intent of nearly all of the newly founded weeklies and dailies. The New York *Yiddishe Zeitung*, for instance, described itself as "socialist and Jewish." This synthesis of socialism and Jewish nationalism was a hybrid product—one that had never flourished on the Jewish scene in eastern Europe. With the hindsight of seventy-five years of development of the Yiddish press, we can see a gradual flattening out of these extreme positions, and a merging of party programs and publications, to the extent of blunting their original political bite. This loss of ideological fervor, whether political or religious, for better and for worse, should probably be regarded as part of the process of Americanization.

The political radicalism of the *Yiddishe Folkszeitung* was evident in its first issue, June 25, 1886, in which its editor, Moses Mintz, declared that the Jewish worker should feel united "with all the workers of the world"—with "the condition of the Jewish worker in the world in general and in America in particular!" Yet solidarity with the working masses was not enough to solve the Jewish problem. "On the battle-line he [the Jewish worker] has many comrades as a worker; as a Jew he has very few. The Jewish problem is very important and needs careful consideration for a proper solution. He will understand the solution only when he is familiar with Jewish history." One might think that a familiarity with Jewish history could also lead to religious conclusions concerning the "end of days" of which the prophets spoke. But this was not the "proper solution" intended by Mintz. His journalistic aim was to shed light on the "labor problem, its development from the beginning to the present, and all the means that have been considered by the learned and outstanding representatives of the labor movement in order to solve that problem." The Jewish problem was to be seen "in relation to the development of culture and civilization among various peoples." In line with this aim, the *Folkszeitung* averred that it would publish articles on "the general development of culture and civilization" and on "movements in Jewish history, written by the outstanding Jewish historians." This combination of educational and political intention was a marked feature not only of the weeklies, but of the dailies as well. In this regard, the Yiddish press was superior to the mass-circulation journalism of the American dailies. To raise the literary taste of its readers and by so doing transform the quality of Yiddish, it constantly printed chapters from forthcoming books and commissioned the writing of novels and short stories.[9]

In the judgment of Sh. Niger, the outstanding literary critic and historian of Yiddish literature, "In Yiddish all literature stemmed from journalism. The newspapers and periodicals reprinted the works of European Yiddish writers, especially Mendele Mocher Seforim's stories and Peretz' stories and poems. They published the works of the new writers who made their debut in America. They were the meeting ground of the novelist, the poet, the critic, and the reader. In the first period of Yiddish literature in America *practically every Yiddish short story, novel, poem, and critical essay appeared first in the press and only later, if at all, in a book.*"

It was in the 1890s that the Yiddish press came into its own. Within one decade the following dailies were founded: the *Vahrheit*, the *Forward*, the *Abend-Blatt*, and the Chicago *Yiddisher Kurier*. All of them battled for the holy cause of secularism and class struggle. New monthlies such as *Die Zukunft* (which

---

[9] Oscar Handlin, *Adventure in Freedom, Three Hundred Years of Jewish Life in America* (New York: McGraw-Hill, 1954): "The emphasis [in the Yiddish press] was therefore on features. There were extensive weekly supplements and the daily editions also gave over much space to stories, poetry, exhortative articles, advice to the lovelorn and the homesick" (p. 127).

still appears today and is probably the best Jewish monthly in any language), *Die Freie Gesellschaft, Die Naie Zeit, Der Naier Geist,* devoted themselves to "literature and the discussion of social problems." These monthlies and the four new weeklies which were established during this period constituted a pioneer venture in adult education that has not been duplicated since. The Yiddish press considered itself to be the educator of the Jewish masses. Despite its partiality to political radicalism and its hostility to Jewish religion, despite its lack of educational continuity and its hectoring tone, it did help to awaken new social and intellectual interests.

There must be some qualification, however, of this universally acknowledged judgment. The propagandistic call to solidarity among members of the working class, the trumpeting of popular ideas of Darwin and Marx, could only lead to a superficial judgment of the future, both political and scientific. The envisioned Utopia based upon enlightenment, natural science, and class struggle was never to be born. The expectation of the Utopia was itself a product of an oversimplified examination of society and human nature. Had there been a viable and relevant religious press during this decade, clear-cut limits could have been set to the vaunting political radicalism of the major portion of the Yiddish press. But such warnings were never sounded. The struggle between the *Tageblatt* and the *Morgen-Zhurnal* (established in 1901) focused solely on the value and origins of religious observances. The religious sector of the Yiddish press never appears to have contested the supremacy of Americanism or American culture. It was therefore led to approach Jewish religious observances (the Sabbath, the dietary laws, and so on) in a spirit either of accommodation (violate one Sabbath, so that you might observe the next), or of intransigency. More often than not, the latter stance was adopted. At the moment it was the easier position; in the long run it was to prove disastrous. If the slightest accommodation to the realities of American life was to be denied and condemned, then the first compromise would cause the collapse of the whole structure of religious observance. For many thousands of religious Jews, this proved to be the case.

The normal cleavage between one generation and the next developed into a state of permanent emotional alienation, in which parental religious observances were seen by the children as impediments to American progress. Because the religious values of the immigrant parents often rested upon simple gnomic convictions, which grew from the soil of the religious tradition and the inbred folk-society existence of eastern Europe, both the values and observances of Judaism were rejected by the native-born second generation. Judaism became equivalent to immigrant culture, and as such could have no significance for the totally new social structure of the United States. The sons and daughters of the eastern European Jewish immigrants were "the weakest link in the chain of Jewish continuity," an "in-between layer . . . which [had] broken with the Jewish past and [had] lost faith in a Jewish future."[10]

Despite the almost bewildering variety of types of Jewish orthodoxy—Ashkenazic, Sephardic, Hasidic, Misnagdic, Lithuanian, Polish, Russian, Galician, Rumanian, and Hungarian—none was able to retain the allegiance of the sons to the religion of their fathers. Since neither the contemporary rabbinate nor the religious sector of the Yiddish press helped to distinguish between folk-society elements and religion, they bear considerable responsibility for the fact that Jewish religious concern in the United States so often is involved with the cult of respectability.

In its heyday (1914–24) the Yiddish press boasted five dailies in New York (*Forward, Tog, Morgen-Zhurnal, Freiheit, Tageblatt*); two in Chicago (*Forward* and *Yiddisher Kurier*); one in

[10] Bezalel Sherman, "Three Generations," *Jewish Frontier*, Vol. XXI, No. 7 (July 1954), p. 229, quoted in Will Herberg, *Protestant—Catholic—Jew*, revised edition (New York: Doubleday/Anchor Books, 1960), p. 184. Also cf. Nathan Glazer, *American Judaism* (Chicago: Chicago University Press, 1957), p. 85: ". . . it was nevertheless true that the overwhelming majority of the immigrants' children had deserted Judaism. They did not convert, but they were either indifferent or hostile to the traditional religion."

Cleveland (*Die Yiddishe Welt*), one in Philadelphia (*Die Yiddishe Welt*), and two in Canada (*Montreal Canada Adler* and *Toronto Yiddischer Zhurnal*). They must not be considered as newspapers (such as *The New York Times*) but as daily magazines. Each of them carried serious articles, essays, stories, poetry, and popular science on a daily basis; indeed, the only two surviving Yiddish dailies (*Forward* and *Tog-Morgen-Zhurnal*) still maintain this policy. All of these papers were and still are staffed by men whom conventional dailies would never employ: poets, short-story writers, and novelists. There were more signed articles than in the conventional American press, but coverage of the news of the day was almost always secondary to the eagerly awaited opinions of a favored columnist. Dated news, reporting of events that occurred one or two days previous to the publication of the paper, was characteristic and can sometimes still be found in the pages of the Yiddish press.

The *Forward* (founded in 1897) was for four generations the lengthened shadow of a remarkable journalist and editor, Abraham Cahan, who died in 1951. He converted the *Forward* from a struggling daily to the most influential and profitable of the Yiddish dailies. The building which houses this paper, and which was constructed from the profits made by his operation, still stands on the Lower East Side of New York. Read by both the working classes and secular Jewish intelligentsia, the *Forward* at times leaned to the sensational; but it always employed such gifted literary artists as Shalom Asch, B. Z. Goldberg, and Mane Leib. This generation has died out. With the gradually accelerating decline in the number of Yiddish readers, it is doubtful whether writers of that calibre can be replaced. Until Cahan's first trip to Palestine in the 1920s, the *Forward* was consistently anti-Zionist and anti-religious. The anti-Zionism was modified somewhat by Cahan's nostalgic tour, and during the 1940s the paper abandoned its negative attitude toward Jewish national aspirations. Although its anti-religious policy is not as strident as in earlier years, its secular orientation has remained constant. Its 65th anniversary edition (December 30, 1962) contained an article by Dr. Zvi Cahn, dismissing Judaism as a "package" of childish beliefs, proclaiming religion to be merely a private matter, and paradoxically limiting religious liberty by two conditions—that the individual cannot exchange Judaism for another religion, nor should he berate the unenlightened pietist.

During the first three decades of the twentieth century, the *Forward* openly linked its coverage of daily news with socialist partisanship. In Cahan's eyes and by reason of his efforts, socialism became the key to the conversion of the Jewish workingman into a Jewish trade unionist. It was a substitute faith to be promulgated with missionary fervor, with a characteristic vision of the world, a philosophy of history, and a springboard for definite action on the social scene: "The role of the *Forward* in the Jewish labor movement, especially during the early days, emphasizes the very important fact that for the Jewish workers of four or five decades ago, Socialism was not so much a social ideology or political creed as a *moral cement* that joined them together into a cohesive force and made collective action possible."[11]

Some indication of the tone and standpoint of the paper in those days can be gained from some quotations from an editorial (July 25, 1915):

> The cloak-makers' difficulty has ended with the complete recognition of the union's rights. What the union claimed all along since the protocol was broken off—namely that the union is strong enough to stand on its own feet without a protocol—that has been confirmed in a splendid, impressive way . . . The union not only has the trade in its hands, not only the sympathy of all workers of America, but public opinion is on its side . . .

> Will the employers dare to disregard the decision of such an arbitration committee? Will they dare to resume the fight with the great, truly mighty union? It is ridiculous.

> And now, that the troubles are over and we are beginning to

11 Will Herberg, "The Jewish Labor Movement in the United States," p. 14.

earn money, let us start to think seriously of the great tragedy of our brethren in Russia. Jewish workers of America! Millions of Jews are being torn to pieces by wild beasts in human form. They are being constantly uprooted from their home.

Begin at once to gather funds, in the same brave, organized way as you carry on your struggles.

The seemingly abrupt coupling of the cloak-makers' strike with the dismal condition of the Jews in Russia was not unusual in either the *Forward* or the other Yiddish dailies. Since the Jewish people was dispersed throughout the world, its national or religious condition was germane to any issue that faced American Jewry. Because news of the Jewish situation was not carried, much less featured, by American dailies, the Yiddish press functioned to enhance the feeling of Jewish solidarity by interweaving news of Jewish communities outside the United States with purely local economic struggles.

During these same years there was also a communist daily, *Di Freiheit,* founded in 1922. It waged unremitting ideological war against socialism and attempted to win away the *Forward* readership, but its circulation never exceeded 40,000. Until the Russian Revolution made bolshevism a live issue for the socialist movement, *Freiheit's* first editor, Moishe Olgin, had been a staff member of the *Forward*. The personal and ideological friendship that existed between Olgin and Cahan was forever severed by the party line generated by Moscow.

Midway in the spectrum between the radicalism of the *Forward* and *Di Freiheit,* and the religious and political conservatism of the *Tageblatt* and *Morgen-Zhurnal,* stood the mildly liberal *Der Tog* (The Day). It was the only one of the New York Yiddish dailies that from its founding actively espoused Zionism, but its editorial position had no direct link with any particular Zionist party. It became the focus of the Yiddishist-Hebraist dispute, and it tried to foster the creation of an indigenous Yiddish-American literature through the promotion of a network of Yiddish schools and the publication of Yiddish books. In this aim it found itself allied with the *Forward*.

Together with the *Tageblatt*, the *Morgen-Zhurnal* constituted the right wing of the Yiddish press. It was established in 1902, by Jacob Saphirstein, to demonstrate that "Orthodox Judaism and patriotic Americanism" were not antagonistic to each other. A contemporary description suggests an interesting picture of this publisher: "Jacob Saphirstein was a man of metropolitan outlook. . . . He was a publisher, a businessman. Tall, well-built, with neatly-combed brown hair over a tall forehead, and a brown Vandyke beard, Saphirstein impressed people with his nimbleness and vivacity. He looked as if he were always in a hurry. He walked briskly, spoke quickly and with sharp gestures, came to quick decisions, and at once proceeded to implement them."[12]

Politically, Saphirstein's paper supported the Republican party. Since it was the only Yiddish daily published during the morning hours, its circulation was always bolstered by the unemployed who eagerly scanned the "help wanted" and "business opportunities" columns. The *Morgen-Zhurnal* was originally anti-Zionist, but Israel Friedkin, who succeeded Saphirstein, combined its pro-religious orientation with Zionism. In 1953 the paper merged with *Der Tog*, and remains one of the two Yiddish dailies still in circulation.

Further insight may be gained into the intense individualism that characterized these papers and their editors during their heyday by this sketch of the contrast between Cahan, editor of the *Forward*, and Peter Wiernik, editor of the *Morgen-Zhurnal:*

> Cahan is radical in his ideas, dynamic, impetuous and somewhat erratic in temperament, never afraid of new innovations, ever the stormy petrel in one fight or another. Wiernik is a Tory, calm, reserved, never given to anger, the most methodical and punctual man I have ever met. While Cahan may be regarded as typical of the Russian intelligentsia that was nour-

[12] Miriam Shomer Zunser, "The Jewish Literary Scene in New York," *Yivo Annual of Social Science*, Vol. VII, 284.

ished on revolutionary ideas, during more than half a century, Wiernik looks, acts, and writes as would a New Englander of the generation of Emerson, Longfellow and Lowell . . . Wiernik is in love with everything American, sees all the virtues of the world embodied in Anglo-Saxondom and no good whatsoever in the Slavs, and never misses an opportunity to chastise the Jewish radical element for its romantic yearnings for the erstwhile land of Czars and pogroms.[13]

With the virtual halting of Jewish immigration in the 1920s, the Yiddish press has declined continually in journalistic vitality and circulation. It never succeeded in capturing the hearts or the attention of the second-generation native-born American Jews. Predictions as to its demise are made with mechanical regularity,[14] but although its influence will be peripheral and its economic condition hazardous, the Yiddish press will probably remain a feature of the American Jewish scene for the foreseeable future. Indeed, should there occur in the near future a large-scale Jewish immigration from Mexico or South America (particularly Argentina), where there is a numerically significant and economically strong Yiddish-speaking population, the circulation figures of the Yiddish press will again skyrocket.

From a religious standpoint, it is the inbred secularism of the Yiddish press, and its compulsive adherence to a nonpluralistic view of American society, that prevents it from becoming an authentic voice. Its ethics are those of the journalistic market place—neither better nor worse. Although its literary standards are considerably higher than those of the general press, its positions on issues of moment to the Jewish community are usually identical with the libertarianism of non-Jewish secularists. On issues such as church-state, provision of federal aid to religious schools, obscenity laws, freedom of expression—the editorial

[13] Philip Rubin, "The Yiddish Press," *American Mercury*, March 1927, pp. 351–52.
[14] The anonymous authority of *Time* recently labeled the *Forward* "an anachronism" (December 28, 1962, p. 46).

columns of the *Forward* and the *Morgen-Zhurnal* sound like echoes of *The Nation* or *The New Republic*. Only when anti-Semitism and the problem of Sunday closing laws come to the fore, can a distinctively Jewish attitude be discerned in the Yiddish press. When George Lincoln Rockwell, a rabidly anti-Semitic "American Nazi," applied for a permit to preach his doctrines in New York on July 4, 1960, both Yiddish dailies came out editorially against granting it. They invoked two arguments in support of their impassioned denial of Rockwell's right of freedom to speak. One was the clear and present danger of a riot in Union Square, the proposed site for Rockwell's demonstration. In this contention they were undoubtedly correct. There are a good many survivors of Nazi concentration camps still resident in New York who could not remain dispassionate in the face of Rockwell's lunatic rallying cry, "Gas the Jews." The second argument of the dailies was that Rockwell's brand of poison should not be allowed to be spewed forth in public. Here the general tradition of interpretation of constitutional guarantees of freedom of speech stands against them; and in June 1961, the Court of Appeals, New York's highest court, affirmed Rockwell's right to speak in New York City.

Since their readership is still centered mainly in lower Manhattan and Brooklyn, the Yiddish dailies are sensitive to any law that would affect the economic fortunes of their readers. A good many of these maintain the Sabbath by closing their shops. In order to recoup their loss in business revenue, they open their doors on Sunday. New York State has a Sunday closing law which is differentially enforced; that is, the selection of items that can be sold in the state on Sunday morning or afternoon (the sale of beer is prohibited until 1:00 P.M. in New York City) is arbitrarily determined. Jewish kosher butchers are especially affected by this law, because the sale of meat is prohibited on Sunday. Appeals from these "blue laws" made in New York and New Jersey were denied by the Supreme Court of the United States. In his majority opinion, Chief Justice Warren contended that although originally a religious day of rest, Sunday had come to be accepted as a national day of rest, without any religious significance in-hering in such inertia.

On this issue the Yiddish dailies opposed the general trend of American society. But they put the justification for keeping Jewish shops open purely on a "fair play" basis: Why should the religiously observant Jewish shopkeeper suffer economically be-cause he celebrates the seventh day, the Biblically ordained Sab-bath, rather than the first, ecclesiastically ordained day of rest? Put in this way, the issue avoids the clash of Jews, Christians, and secularists about the significance of the Sabbath. The formal re-ligious issue is thus never joined. By tacitly assuming the position of civil libertarians, the Yiddish press avoided having to raise the embarrassing question as to what the position of the religious Jew might be were the Sabbath laws of the State of Israel to be challenged by a nonobservant Israeli. In Israel, regardless of private conviction on the matter, all commercial establishments are closed on the Sabbath. The hebdomadal rhythm of the re-ligious life is, for all intents and purposes, part of the national life. What the religious Jew would affirm in Israel would be denied by him in America, where the invocation of a strict interpretation of the doctrine of separation of church and state has led to the divorce of religion from politics. By responding to the lure of a secular interpretation of the social order, instead of shaping and giving expression to the values of the religious community, the Yiddish press (and here it shares its guilt with the English-Jewish press) proved derelict.

Because religious values have often been propounded by a creative minority, it might be possible to see in the Yiddish press the potential for comprehensive expression of a religious judg-ment on the emptiness and hedonistic materialism of American society. But one would have to look very hard to justify this hope. The Yiddish press still lives off the memory of past glories, and sighs nostalgically for the golden age when Jews were prole-tarian immigrants or exemplary echoes of a European style of piety.

THE ENGLISH-JEWISH PRESS:
ITS SCOPE AND
CURRENT TECHNICAL PROBLEMS

With the battle of acculturation won, the Yiddish press lost the rationale for its continued existence as the dominant religious and cultural force among American Jews. The entire "problematic" of immigrant life had now disappeared. No longer could Yiddish newspapers rely upon intellectual and emotional sympathy from their readers in muckraking over "sweatshop" conditions; the demand for a daily lesson in American civics and modes of behavior dropped precipitously with the rise of the generation of native-born American Jews. The linkage of the reader to "the other side—the old country" simply evaporated. As a pivotal social and educational force the Yiddish press had accomplished its task—well, if not always wisely.

Moreover, the physical makeup of the American Jewish community has changed, at first gradually, and then with ever-increasing acceleration, in the four decades between the 1920s and the 1960s. At first concentrated in a few urban centers (New York, Chicago, Boston, Baltimore, Detroit), the Jewish community has tended to move outward toward the suburbs. In this movement it has displayed in but concentrated form the abandonment of the central city on the part of upwardly mobile non-Jewish Americans. The relatively close-knit American Jewish community of the era 1900–1920 has become a geographic ghost. The "Jewish masses" which could be mustered for protest marches, indignation meetings, and political pressure are almost impossible to locate today. The economic reason for this transformation is not difficult to cite. The shift of Jewish population outside the larger metropolitan areas is almost entirely due to the middle-income status achieved by most American Jews, which has had enormous effects on every area crucial to the Jewish community—education, religion, anti-discrimination activities, interfaith work; indeed, in every area of community concern.

Despite its geographic dispersion and the decline in its major medium of communication (the Yiddish press), the American Jewish community still manifests the twin lineaments of a community—consensus and concern. Both of these indicators, however, exhibit a range and variation that is bewildering to the uninformed observer. In religion, indeed, precious little consensus is discernible. American Jews have been fractionalized into denominations—Conservative, Orthodox, Reform, and Reconstructionist—each with a different stance toward the religious tradition, and with different expectations of Jewish destiny. Between them they provide for approximately half the American Jewish population; the other half is uncommitted, secular-humanist, or apathetic in religious matters.

The four major religious groupings have produced a denominational English-Jewish press which is growing in influence and circulation. Representative publications include the annual *Yearbook of the Central Conference of American Rabbis* (Reform) and the *Proceedings of the Rabbinical Assembly of America* (Conservative), published in English and Hebrew; *American Judaism* (Reform), *United Synagogue Review* (Conservative), and *Jewish Life* (Orthodox), which are monthlies directed to laymen. There are also the professional rabbinical journals: *Conservative Judaism* and the *CCAR Journal* appear quarterly, while the Orthodox *Tradition* is a biannual. Biweekly magazines such as *Our Age* (Conservative) and *Keeping Posted* (Reform) are circulated to teen-agers affiliated with the synagogues; the only biweekly of intellectual stature is *The Reconstructionist*, whose influence extends far beyond its somewhat limited circulation.

Although the figure is to be treated with reserve, it is believed that there are some 4,500 Jewish congregations in the United States. At least 1,500 of them issued weekly or fortnightly synagogue bulletins, which constitute a periodical genre *sui generis*. An impressionistic content analysis of 300 of these bulletins yielded the following result: news of synagogue activities (worship, social gatherings, education of the young, organizational affiliates) used up 75 per cent of available space; advertising,

10 per cent; the digest of the rabbi's Sabbath sermon and/or message to members from its spiritual leader, 5 per cent; listing of donors to various synagogue funds,[15] 10 per cent.

Since such periodicals constitute the chief instrument of communication between synagogue leadership (lay or rabbinic) and congregational members, this spectrum of content is discouraging. The fundamental weakness of the congregational bulletin is its evident parochialism. Rarely are readers urged to turn their gaze from organizational trivia to issues that are crucial from a religious point of view. A consideration of the vexing problem of church-state relations in a modern pluralistic society, or an exploration of the resources of Jewish tradition as applicable to social or national problems—these simply do not occur in these bulletins. Insofar as this lacuna is tolerated or supported, the congregational weeklies (and biweeklies) have failed in their educational responsibilities. With the exception of the two monthly congregational bulletins (those of the Brooklyn Jewish Center and the Temple Israel, Great Neck, Long Island) whose contents include "think pieces," the above judgment applies to every synagogue bulletin this observer has seen. They are house organs in the most primitive sense of the word.

A somewhat similar, if more qualified, critique can be made of the journalistic and religious quality of the denominational publications. The congregational bulletins are edited in a rudimentary fashion by the printer. Hence their sometimes slapdash appearance. On the other hand, publications such as the *United Synagogue Review, American Judaism,* and *Jewish Life,* which together reach almost a million readers, are excellently edited. In terms of layout and picture journalism, they compare favorably with mass-circulation magazines. Although they are occasionally garish or self-consciously arty in their cover photos and drawings, their journalistic expertise is of a high order.

The content of these journals, however, does not match the

15 One congregation listed some twenty-eight separate funds, each named in honor of a deceased member, and whose money supported a separate and distinct synagogue project!

technical skill with which they are put together. Editorial focus is so wide as to be meaningless. Many of the articles are of the "how to" variety—how to run a synagogue membership campaign, how to increase attendance at worship services or how to listen to the rabbi's sermon. There is also the constant note of group self-congratulation: "we hail" the establishment of a particular branch of the movement in a distant city or country, or the achievements of our last synagogue or temple convention. Such material might better be relegated to a community service division of each of the denominational groups. The continued emphasis that the Union of American Hebrew Congregations, the United Synagogue of America, and the Union of Orthodox Jewish Congregations place upon this kind of journalistic content makes the religious concern of synagogue-affiliated Jews seem petty. There is no extended treatment or critical analysis of how Judaism can and should affect civil society. One does find, however, an occasional restatement of religion's right to "meddle" in the affairs of civil society:

> The question is raised frequently as to why a synagogue such as ours takes a stand . . . in such worldly matters as the McCarran-Walter immigration law, or segregation, or any broad problem confronting our country or community . . . We cannot speak for any other synagogue organization or move-ment within Judaism but we believe that this applies to all of us as Jews: At the very core of Judaism is its concern for Social Justice. Torah, the prophetic teachings, the Talmud, our liturgy, literally breathe it. We do not "meddle" when we point out injustices of one kind or another in our society. It is our duty. It is the mandate of Judaism.[16]

This is in many ways a brave and noble statement. But it casts little or no light on the proper contours of our society, or the role religion is to play in it. It would also have been worth asking

[16] *United Synagogue Review,* Spring, 1958, p. 3.

what rights the civil order of the United States possesses in relation to Jewish religious institutions.

A content analysis of the major publications of the Union of American Hebrew Congregations, Union of Orthodox Jewish Congregations, and the United Synagogue of America would prove helpful—and perhaps revealing—at this point. The circulation figures of the Conservative and Reform publications, *American Judaism* and the *United Synagogue Review,* are quite respectable, the former reaching 200,000 subscribers and the latter 175,000. A circulation problem does not exist, for subscription to the magazines is automatic when one joins the individual synagogue or temple. A judgment as to the effectiveness of these journals is difficult, however, for there has been no research on the impact they have had upon their readers.

The cover of the Spring, 1962 issue of *American Judaism* is a piece of original art work by Shalom of Galilee. Although many Reform rabbis complain privately that the expenditure of precious funds for the commissioning of "arty" magazine covers is wasteful, it seems clear that the formation of aesthetic taste in ritual objects, synagogue architecture, and book design cannot be relegated to separate publications as is the case in American Protestantism. Since *American Judaism* is sponsored, however, by both the Union of American Hebrew Congregations *and* its affiliates (the National Federation of Temple Brotherhoods, the National Federation of Temple Sisterhoods, the National Federation of Temple Youth, the National Association of Temple Administrators, and the National Association of Temple Educators), the package nature of the publications promotes a rather uneasy combination of modern art and public relations photographs. We are greeted in this issue with pictures of the granting of assorted awards, diplomas, degrees, citations, pins, plaques, medals, trophies, books, and insignia by and to various key figures in the Reform movement. Indeed, of the sixty-three pages in this particular issue of the magazine, twenty-five pages, constituting more than a third of its contents, are devoted to organizational news of this kind. The magazine is heavy with advertisements which occupy

two-thirds of each of the final twelve pages, thus further cutting
into the amount of space available for responsible religious journalism. The masthead lists a staff of six, the largest of the three
magazines under consideration but nevertheless smaller than that
of a comparable Protestant journal.

The first article is strictly of the "we hail" type—a salute to
organizational expansion curiously entitled "A New Judaism in
Israel." The new Judaism, apparently, "is characterized by the
family pew, the organ, and an original liturgy utilizing selections
from several liberal prayerbooks, translations [from English into
Hebrew presumably] from the Union Prayerbook, spiritual poetry, and original prayers. Its theology reflects a point of view
consistent with that of other World Union congregations throughout the world" (p. 6). This is rather a comedown from the old
Judaism in which, in the Hebrew idiom, there is no word for
"religion." It would seem that Reform Judaism, which has always
proclaimed itself to be "prophetic" rather than "rabbinic" in
origin and intent, concentrates on worship when exporting itself
to the Holy Land. Although the author decries the "constrictive
bind [sic!] yoking religion and the Israel state," and hints sagely
that Reform will "one day play a critical role" in the solution
of this problem, there is no indication anywhere in the article that
for the Hebrew Bible there was anything other than an indis-
soluble connection between piety and politics. Although American Reform is the new Judaism, it apparently needs Israel Reform
for its own rejuvenation: "Outside of North America, Liberal
congregations are in an arrested or struggling position. Only in
Israel are there prospects of a colorful and creative movement
likely to pour new ideas and forms and zest into the stream of
Reform worship and theology."

Among the other articles, we find a clever homily on the life
of Joseph, then a double-page photographic spread on the first
congregation for the deaf on the East Coast, followed by a
Broadway producer's reflections on producing his play, *The Wall*,
in Munich, and a short story by a talented young novelist. The
remaining articles are equally diverse, including a brief but none-

theless banal exploration of Jewish humor, a first-rate theater review by David Boroff, a rambling survey of four books by Reform rabbis, and a religious view of civil defense that depends more on psychiatry than the prophets.

Especially revealing is an article responding to an earlier piece by Philip Roth, who had assaulted reader sensibilities in the Winter, 1961 issue by insisting that the writings of Harry Golden and Leon Uris were banal, inconsequential, sentimental, and slick. Roth had obviously touched a raw nerve, since his antagonist is driven to make such incredible statements as, "If Hamlet had possessed just one-tenth of Ari Ben Canaan's resolution and unswerving purpose, Shakespeare would have been a much richer and more successful man!" Although Jewish tradition adjures Jews to remember the example of Abraham, who began his career by breaking his father's idols, and insists that the Jew remain faithful to God only insofar as he recalls the command, "Thou shalt not make unto thyself a graven image," the author rhapsodizes that the new image of the Jew as muscular hero, "being historically true and psychologically sound, is of great value to the Jewish people if only for the reason that it nourishes the self-image of ourselves and our children. It imbues us with courage, it makes us feel worthy, it instills in us hope, and it gives us the will to fight for a better life."

The *United Synagogue Review* has a different organizational slant, but the same basic direction as *American Judaism*. It is produced by a staff of four people; its budget is severely limited so that independent articles and art work cannot be commissioned, as is the case with its more affluent counterpart. Also, unlike *American Judaism*, it does not attempt to lump within the covers of a single magazine the organizational concerns of its sisterhood, men's clubs, youth groups, educators, and administrators. These groups have their own publications; nevertheless, the *Review* devotes nine of the thirty-two pages of its Winter, 1963 issue to reports of organizational appointments, elections, advancements, and techniques. Of these, three consist of letters to the editor, including one from an eleven-year-old girl who "fell in love with the photographs," and a single example of mild criticism.

Articles are drawn from convention orations, publicity releases, and acquaintances of the editor. Since his only inducement to prospective contributors is, "Think of the number of the readers that you will reach with your article!" well-known writers, novelists, and poets rarely, if ever, make their appearance in the *Review*. Three of the five articles in the Winter issue are purely institutional in their concern. One describes in glowing terms the growth of the United Synagogue Youth movement (organization of teen-agers) and Atid, a newly founded organization for college students. Institutional affiliation appears as the chief goal of the latter: "Atid's programs are geared specifically to the needs, abilities, and interests of college-age youth. Sustained by this activity during their college careers and into their middle twenties, members are expected to be ripe for full-fledged synagogue membership as young adults." In a world caught up in conflict and confusion, this is a somewhat less than inspiring goal for a national organization of collegians.

On the other hand, there is one exciting confrontation of three writers on "The Young Jew: Conflict and Counsel." A father, son, and uncle speak of their relationship to the ancestral heritage: the son, a college student at Cornell, is obviously at sea about the ideas and beliefs of Judaism; the uncle is a convinced proponent of Jewish secularism; and the father is a staunch protagonist of "the synagogue way." (Why not "the Jewish way"?) It is noteworthy that the father's article refers continually to specifics about the synagogue as an institution, but speaks of the ideas and beliefs which it incorporates in ambiguous fashion:

> Judaism as a religion has an intellectual relevance, and unless we discover it, our Jewish heritage will remain an affair of insignificance, without bearing on life's central issues. And it is in the synagogue that relevance is best discovered, for it is on the synagogue that it has proved to be most firmly and cogently based . . . . To be a Jew means to be committed to

certain basic ideas; not only to perform certain actions at certain times, but to stand for certain principles at all times. And it is only from the synagogue that Jews have been able to draw the courage and the resolution to nourish those principles and those ideas.

But the synagogue does not occupy the same position vis-à-vis its members as the Church does to its communicants; the holy community—that is, the Jewish people in its corporate life—is the primary although not the ultimate focus of religious concern. The article seems to suggest that in many minds institutionalism has displaced theology; for example, there is a good deal of discussion of ritual, but without reference to its ultimate grounding in commitment to the covenant with God and the responsibility to sanctify His name.

The remaining articles can be dismissed quickly. "Final Honors for Sacred Books" is a piece of Jewish exotica, depicting how children in the religious school of a Philadelphia congregation set about burying worn-out Bibles and prayerbooks. There is more than an occasional note of cuteness, and we become aware that technique can be an end in itself when a page consists of 150 words of copy and two photographs bled into the margin. A review of an important book, of equal relevance to biblical studies and religious phenomenology, is contributed by a member of the department of homiletics at The Jewish Theological Seminary. Limitations of space provide no opportunity for critique and evaluation.

Jewish Life (originally *Orthodox Jewish Life*) is the lay publication of the Union of Orthodox Jewish Congregations and appears on a bimonthly basis. It has a staff of six; in appearance and format it is akin to the *Reader's Digest*, and crowds its print onto the page without editorial subheads. The April, 1962 issue contains five articles, two pieces of short fiction, one book review, and three "departments" (two hardly deserve the name—one is the ubiquitous "letters to the editor" section, and the other presents a brief biographical rundown of the writers appearing in that issue).

Jewish Life does manage to exclude organizational trivia, and for this it deserves commendation. The articles may be outrageously slanted toward the unassailability of Orthodoxy, and its journalistic style is hardly professional, but its articles are packed with facts. "Human Slaughter In New Jersey," for instance, is a full report on pending legislation that would have the effect of banning the slaughter of cattle in consonance with Jewish ritual prescriptions. "Anglo-Jewry in Orbit" is a lengthy report of the struggle for power now going on between the Chief Rabbi of Great Britain on the one hand, and Rabbi Louis Jacobs and the *London Jewish Chronicle* on the other, for control of the principalship of England's foremost rabbinical seminary, Jews College. Since the author of the article is himself on the editorial board of the *London Jewish Chronicle's* newly launched competitor, the *Jewish Tribune*, one should not expect impartiality in the treatment of the dispute. The remaining articles, "The Space-Age Cult of Practicality," "The Indian Jews of Mexico," and "The Young in Triangular Perspective," have touches of the exhortative but are sufficiently ballasted with facts to maintain interest. The fiction and the book review are quite second-rate. The homilies, supplied in each issue by the industrious executive vice-president of the organization, can only be described as lugubrious.

Although the confusion is not now as great as it was ten years ago, these synagogue organs display the common syndrome of pausing on two thresholds. They must allot space to organizational advancement and reinforcement, for it was to fill this need that they were originally produced. Once they are properly budgeted and staffed, however, this "service" type of orientation has to become secondary, lest these publications lapse into the category of ordinary trade journals. Fortunately certain ideological emphases have been muted somewhat in recent years. The popular view of religion in the 1950s, as a promoter of congenial family relations, as an aid to individual psychological adjustment, and as a social agent designed to foster the survival of the Jews as a group entity, is slowly and with some difficulty disappearing. But no serious assessment of the role of Jewish religion in modern American society has arisen to replace it.

The 1947 report by the Commission on the Freedom of the Press is apposite at this point. According to the Commission, what American society needs from its press today is: "1) a truthful, comprehensive, and intelligent account of the day's events in a context which gives them meaning; 2) a forum for the exchange of comment and criticism; 3) a means of projecting the opinions and attitudes of the groups in the society to one another; 4) a method of presenting and clarifying the goals and values of the society; and 5) a way of reaching every member of the society by the currents of information, thought, and feeling which the press supplies."

Not all of these criteria are applicable equally to the press which we are now considering. It is almost impossible to secure a comprehensive account of newsworthy Jewish religious events. There is no English-Jewish daily newspaper, either secular or religious. The major Jewish news agency, the Jewish Telegraphic Agency, provides both the denominational and a-denominational press with news and feature articles. Despite a career dating back to 1919, however, it is woefully inefficient with regard to news of Jewish religious institutions. Because of its financial dependence upon the Jewish Agency, American Section, items about Israel and Zionist affairs receive top priority in ordering the flow of available news. The raising of communal funds for relief and rehabilitation would seem to be the main business and spiritual armature of American Jews, if one is to take seriously the number of news items devoted to this matter by the Jewish Telegraphic Agency. A complete and comprehensive presentation of what is actually happening in Jewish communities in the United States and abroad is still needed. If the agency were to become a quasi-public enterprise, sponsored and financially supported by all of the varied religious and secular groupings within American Jewry, the texture and type of news published by the

JTA would be quite different from the patterning of events now presented. It should be noted that the *London Jewish Chronicle's* news service, which maintains the high journalistic standards of its sponsor, is beginning to goad the Jewish Telegraphic Agency into greater coverage of religious news events. To this date no major change can be detected.

The denominational lay quarterlies and the rabbinical periodicals do provide forums for the exchange of comment and criticism. The quality of the religious press itself, however, is never the target for a balanced professional critique. Because the information available is both gathered in an impressionistic fashion, and presented with diffuseness and imprecision of purpose, no careful consideration has been given to the third criterion of the Freedom of the Press report. The very posing of the question of who is to project the attitudes and opinions of Jews to other groups in our society is of paramount importance. Here the religious press can have a decisive impact, but as of now nothing has been done on this score. A chorus of dissonant voices reflecting the ideological stance and organizational interest of the American Jewish Committee, the American Jewish Congress, the B'nai B'rith Anti-Defamation League, and the Jewish War Veterans is always heard on national and local affairs. By what right do they speak for the Jewish community, to what purpose, and with what effect? The denominational quarterlies, lay and rabbinic, are the proper forum for airing this explosive question, for the a-denominational press is timid and apprehensive when it comes to this issue.

Since Judaism does not advise indifference to mundane affairs, Jewish religious publications should be concerned with such matters as housing, wages and hours, and public services. In the words of one of the Hassidic masters, "Why do you worry about my soul and your body? It is better that you should worry about my body and your soul!" To sermonize on the dignity of man, without influencing society toward actual implementation and maintenance of that dignity, is a travesty of the Jewish religious conscience. Yet the goals and values of American society remain generally unexamined in Jewish periodicals. Whether there is such a palpable force as "the National Purpose," or whether America is irreducibly pluralistic, along with the implications of the answer to this question, has not been discussed in depth.

Nevertheless, there are good reasons to hope for better things. With the achievement of organizational goals and increased bureaucratic efficiency, the denominational press will increasingly be forced to a consideration of religious issues of substance.[17] The pressure of the non-Jewish press will also be felt as a goad in this direction. The very dynamism of American society will generate a considerable number of issues of sufficient religious concern to compel their consideration by both lay and rabbinic journals.

THE A-DENOMINATIONAL WEEKLIES

At the present time there are forty-five English-Jewish weeklies covering forty cities in twenty-six states. Although it would be inaccurate and overblown to claim that they are "the spiritual guardian of Judaism in America,"[18] they do serve to mediate to the American Jewish community Jewish news that does not appear in the general press. All of these papers are serviced by the Jewish Telegraphic Agency, whose limitations and general orientation have already been discussed. Although many of these papers serve distinct regions within the United States, it is hard to detect any regional flavor in the papers themselves. There is a flatness of tone and editorial comment, and the lack of regional features tends to make them indistinguishable one from another. Aside from news items of purely local interest, it would be very difficult to realize that one weekly originated in the far West,

[17] Cf. David W. Silverman, "Large-Scale Organization in Jewish Religious Life," *Ethics and Progress*, ed. Harlan Cleveland and Harold B. Lasswell (New York: Harper & Row, Publishers, 1962), pp. 213–35.

[18] Philip Slomovitz, "The English-Jewish Press in America," *The Jewish Journalist*, London, December, 1961, pp. 4–5. This is the only jarring note in an article marked by scholarship and insight.

while another serves a southern Jewish community. There is no program for the development of local writing talent; and in many Jewish communities the production of the newspaper becomes a one-man or one-family operation. Some notion of the lack of professional competence in the Jewish press is seen in this account of its early days:

> Apart from certain exceptions in several of the larger communities, newspapers were served by men who supplemented their activities in the rabbinate, social work, and related fields. In most cases persons from other fields or those who were temporarily dislocated drifted toward these periodicals. Here and there some of the recruits had previous general experience, but in most instances the newcomers were amateurs, which only denotes limitations and is not necessarily a term of reproach. In a sense, then, the Jewish press just happened. It came into being because of the urge for expression felt by founders and leaders of the community.[19]

The a-denominational weeklies have never transcended their origins; nearly all of them began as social and family journals. The *rites de passage*—birth, circumcision, *bar mitzvah*, engagement, marriage, illness, and death—originally confined to the home and synagogue, were announced in these journals for the information of friends and relations. The curse of the congregational bulletins—the avid desire to see one's name in print—gave birth to the a-denominational weeklies and in most cases (with the exception of the JTA news and feature releases) kept them at this level. Although it would be unfair to characterize the weeklies as "gossip gazettes," there are issues (usually December and June, the favored months for weddings) in which the plethora of social items rivals the hard news in space allotted.

The one exception to this judgment is the *National Jewish Post and Opinion,* which publishes editions in Indianapolis (its head-

[19] Bernard G. Richards, "Our English-Jewish Press," *Congress Bi-Weekly,* December 19, 1960, p. 19.

quarters), New York, Chicago, and Los Angeles. Although it pretends to national coverage, it, too, relies upon the Jewish Telegraphic Agency and the *London Jewish Chronicle* for its news sources. Local correspondents in the cities mentioned above act as part-time "stringers" for the paper. Unfortunately the *Post and Opinion* errs on the side of sensationalism; its boldface headlines are at times distortions of the content of the news. Too much importance is attached to items of a bizarre nature. Perhaps this sensationalism is but the reaction to the official news purveyed by the JTA, where news, if not already dated, is routine and oversimplified.

A weekly journal, however, whether Jewish or general, has the opportunity—and responsibility—to view the news in some degree of depth, and to focus upon it the light of an informed and discriminating mind, with a specific point of view. Such interpretive analysis of the news would help to provide both unity and form, but the *Post and Opinion* lacks this journalistic catalyst. The editor's lengthy column on the editorial page usually consists of an account of his wanderings from place to place, the people he has spoken to, the sights that he has seen. At times interesting, occasionaly infuriating, the column does not help put the events of the week into any coherent pattern. There is more than adequate space for letters to the editor, but the hodgepodge of pugnaciously held opinions, and the varieties of English styles that are exhibited there, do not fulfill the requirements of "a forum for the exchange of comment and criticism."

The a-denominational weeklies are subject to the same economic and social pressures which have decimated the ranks of the general press. Radio and television have made great inroads on the advertising revenue which it once received. Moreover, community stature among Jews is more often conferred by the mention of one's name in *The New York Times* than by a citation in the English-Jewish press. This exclusion of the English-Jewish press from its proper status-conferring functions has been assailed with bitterness and justice by Philip Slomovitz, the editor of the Detroit *Jewish News*:

. . . the Jews of New York depend for their major Jewish facts upon either *The New York Times* or the several other New York non-Jewish dailies. Perhaps it is primarily a result of this that the publicity directors of national organizations have made it their major goal to strive for "coverage" in *The New York Times* . . . . This striving for space in the *Times* to the exclusion of the Jewish press has become so repulsive that it has assumed the proportions of a *mania*. As a result, the English-Jewish press has been neglected, and the very people who should have made the English-Jewish press their major concern look upon it with contempt—because they have a *Times* to aspire to.

But the justice of this indictment is, after all, truncated. It is not the Jewish public relations men who determine editorial policy and set journalistic standards. Good writing is something that an editor can cultivate only by prudent selection and, sometimes, by outright rejection of articles. Advertising revenue and news tips did not stream to *The New York Times*, for example, *before* it became a newspaper noted for the quality of its coverage and its editorial tone. A good newspaper featuring good writing and coverage can make money in the United States. A daily or weekly with slipshod journalistic standards and an incoherent attitude toward news selection is bound to lose money. To convince Jewish advertisers that space in English-Jewish weeklies is either profitable or rewarding is impossible, granted the journalistic quality of most of the current weeklies. Editorial talent of the order of Abraham Cahan, Hillel Rogoff, or Sh. Dingol, the latter two still active in the Yiddish press, is the one item most needed and sorely absent from the English-Jewish press.

During the summer of 1962, *Our Age* magazine ran a survey of the English-Jewish weeklies, two-thirds of whose editors responded to queries on news coverage, problems, and the outlook for the future. The results encourage no optimism.

An editor in Illinois said the future was "not particularly

bright," while a Tennessee editor summed up his reactions in four words: "Survival of the fittest." A Wisconsin editor opined that "there is a place—and necessity—for a Jewish press. Whether it can survive the fierce competition for advertising remains to be seen." A Georgia editor found that "the outlook is good for a community-controlled press, dim for independents, except in a few population centers."

Editor Joseph G. Weisberg claimed that the Jewish press is "the stepchild" of the American Jewish community which "gives it nothing but expects everything in return." He has some harsh words for the Jewish businessman who "rushes to get into print news and pictures dealing with family *simchas* [joyous events]— and even with his election to lodge office—but then refuses to subscribe to the paper because there is too much social news, and says he doesn't really need to advertise in the paper because Jews don't buy goods, they just read."

One of the really disheartening developments in the Jewish press is the recent acquisition by the United Federation in Pittsburgh of the local English-Jewish weeklies. A similar takeover occurred in St. Louis. Public or communal ownership of local weeklies has the tendency to stifle criticism and encourage cultural and religious *gleichshaltung*. Wide-ranging criticism is desperately needed at the present time; independent ownership is the necessary, if not sufficient, condition for such criticism. Because it is controlled by outside interest, a community-controlled newspaper would become an entertainer but not a teacher.

The most informed reaction to federation ownership came in the reply given by the *Jewish Advocate,* of Massachusetts, to a recent survey arranged by *Our Age*:

> An independent Jewish press is essential to an informed, responsive, and vibrant Jewish community. Every people must have a voice and a source of objective information. The [regular American] dailies cannot serve all the cultures that make up American pluralistic society. The Jewish papers will be as strong as each community which they serve makes them. They

should be privately and not community-owned in order to insure the greatest possible objectivity, and not be controlled by transitory leadership.

THE A-DENOMINATIONAL MONTHLIES

Although thirty-three English-language monthlies, ranging from *The Jewish Farmer* to the *Jewish Digest,* are published in the United States, only two merit our sustained notice—*The Jewish Spectator,* and *Commentary.* Of the two, the latter is the most advanced in terms of substance, and towers over the entire press, denominational and a-denominational, in its technique and style. Graced by a generous subvention from its sponsor, the American Jewish Committee, *Commentary* has consistently maintained a high standard of editorial excellence. Under the editorship of Elliot Cohen it helped spark a minor theological revival among religiously concerned Jews. Religious existentialism found a hospitable domicile in its pages, and the great dislocation of the American Jewish community from the urban areas to the suburbs was richly and significantly reported. The aid of Jewish scholars was enlisted to select and translate portions of the literary and religious heritage which were of relevance to modern concerns. These selections were published in a separate section entitled "From the Cedars of Lebanon."

Under its present editor, Norman Podhoretz, the level of editorial excellence has gone even higher. Symposia on Western values, the dilemma of nuclear warfare, and the nature of the modern economy all were marked by insight and taste. This is in keeping with *Commentary's* Statement of Aims, to be "a journal of significant thought and opinion on Jewish affairs and contemporary issues." Under Podhoretz's editorship, however, a content analysis will disclose that the contemporary issues have received much greater emphasis than Jewish affairs. In the aforementioned symposia, the relevance and resources of Jewish religious tradition were completely and thoroughly slurred. Occasionally *Commentary* serves as gadfly to the religious community. Its April, 1962 issue brought together the surprisingly unlearned and almost completely negative reactions of young Jewish writers and intellectuals to their ethnic origin and religious heritage. The selection of contributors for this issue, presumably the result of Podhoretz's editorial decision, outraged religious sensibilities. As rabbinic critics were not slow to point out, there were enough young intellectuals of Jewish descent whose linkage to their faith was strong and articulate to merit their inclusion in the symposium. Himself convinced that Jewish religion had ceased to speak to the modern age, and in principle could not do so, Podhoretz selected essayists who largely mirrored his point of view. Nevertheless, the symposium served to stimulate much useful reflection; religious leaders, whatever their feelings of outrage, became increasingly aware of the problems of religious education, and of its rather inglorious impact upon a new generation.

The Jewish Spectator is a fiercely independent projection of its woman editor-publisher, Trude Weiss-Rosmarin. Unlike *Commentary*, whose income is assured, and whose solicitation of good writers is practically unlimited, *The Jewish Spectator* depends upon circulation alone for its maintenance. Although at times wrong-headed and fiercely partisan, the *Spectator* does not remain aloof from congregational life, as does its better-endowed competitor. *Commentary* editorializes by selection and emphasis; the *Spectator's* issues are sometimes one-quarter editorial matter, written and pounded home by its editor-publisher. The *Spectator* is the only Jewish journal of importance that has called for a revision of the Jewish community's stand vis-à-vis the church-state question. In its May and September 1962 issues, it courageously called for a dissent from the strict secular libertarian line that had been followed by Jewish defense agencies for the past thirty years. In her editorials, Mrs. Rosmarin threw cold water on the jubilation of the American Jewish defense agencies at the six-to-one ruling of the Supreme Court against constitutionality of the New York Regents prayer. Without assaulting the legality of the decision, the *Spectator* pointed out that Jews constituted only 3 per cent of the American population, and as such should not interfere with the "way of life of the majority":

> This does not mean that Jews should not demand and defend their constitutional rights. It means, however, that they should recognize that the unwritten law of the *force majeure* of the majority is a reality and a fact of life which the minority has to contend with and to respect.

Although a hasty judgment and in my opinion an indefensible one, this statement does mark a growing dissent, felt among rabbis and Jewish laymen, from the Jewish defense-agency position on church-state relations. The Regents prayer decision, and the continuing debate on federal aid to parochial schools, will now *for the first time* force the range of the Jewish press, denominational and a-denominational, to a consideration of the complex question of Judaism's relation to the free society. This would be a service both to the free society and to Judaism.

PROSPECTS AND PROBLEMS

The general vacuity and religious aimlessness of the denominational and a-denominational press has, I think, been made abundantly clear in the preceding pages. The slipshod journalistic standards, and the absence of critical comment on the American Jewish scene from a religious point of view need not be considered, however, as necessarily permanent characteristics. What is needed is some measure of courage, combined with journalistic discrimination and taste, on the part of an editor who is well schooled in Jewish religious values and skillful as a serpent in attracting financial support. Since the weight of the denominational bureaucracy in American Judaism is, in my opinion, not as heavy as that in Protestantism and Catholicism, such a person can arise even within the denominational hierarchy.

In the a-denominational press there are some stirrings toward critical evaluation of American Judaism, but the avowedly secular aims of such publications as *Midstream*, and *Congress Bi-Weekly*, prevent them from becoming a religious pivot for the American Jew. *Midstream*, a quarterly sponsored by the Theodor Herzl Foundation, is officially "a Zionist publication, committed to free inquiry," and in its statement of purpose hopefully calls "for a re-examination of basic concepts and the way to Jewish fulfillment." This statement is somewhat confusing, since Zionism was originally offered as an answer to the "Jewish problem," though in secular and mainly political form. The fact that the Zionist answer has been found wanting, and that speculative feelers are now being extended toward new solutions, is indicative of the current Jewish situation in the United States and Israel. *Congress Bi-Weekly*, sponsored by the American Jewish Congress, is a well-edited though none too lively journal; stringent limitations of space make it difficult for its articles to have much impact.

The case is somewhat different with *Judaism*, a quarterly sponsored in part by the American Jewish Congress. In the past, this journal has provided its readership (consisting mainly of rabbis) with solid pieces of Jewish scholarship and historical research—marred by more than occasional typographical and editorial errors. The magazine appeared to have no discernible focus or stance, but this situation is now being corrected; changes both in format and editorial orientation have been made by the new editor, Steven Schwarzschild.

One glaring lacuna remains both in our analysis and in the kinds of publications sponsored by American Jews. If the task of the Yiddish press was to "escort the Jewish immigrant out of the Eastern European ghetto . . . lead him into modern society, teach him the thought and politics of Western democracy, and, above all, make him an American,"[20] then it succeeded beyond its wildest expectations. The American Jew became so Americanized

[20] Ronald Sanders, "The Jewish Daily Forward," *Midstream*, December 1962, p. 79.

that he deserted the Yiddish language and the newspapers printed in that tongue. The present crisis of the Yiddish press is one of circulation, not of literary quality. On the other hand, the nature of the tasks facing American Jewry during the next five decades is radically different from that of the past fifty years. The American Jew has attained a relatively secure middle-class niche on the social scene. But the American Jewish community is almost completely unaware of the subtle but ongoing pressures toward "columnization" now becoming apparent in American life.

In a provocative analysis, Gerhard Lenski pointed to the fact that:

> American society is moving (though admittedly slowly) towards a "compartmentalized society" of the type found in contemporary Holland and Lebanon . . . In these societies *most of the major institutional systems are obliged to take account of socio-religious distinctions* [italics added]. Hence, political parties, families, sports teams, and even business establishments are often identified with one or another of the major groups, The Dutch even have a word, *verzuiling*, to describe this kind of social arrangement. Literally translated it means "columnization" since society is organized like a series of parallel columns or pillars.[21]

Although Jews have been accustomed to thinking of their own religion in civilizational terms, viz., that religion was but one, albeit central, component of the complex called "Judaism," it has come as a distinct surprise that *church* affiliation has bred the multivalent influences and social forces that Lenski explored with so much insight. This crystallization of activities, associations, groups, and systems poses twin problems—of communication and co-operation. The problem of co-operation among groups in a columnized society is crucial; without it, the social fabric would be ripped and slashed by antagonism and misunder-

[21] *Op. cit.*, p. 365.

standing. In order to secure co-operation, communication among the "columns" must be fostered by the leadership of each of the organized socioreligious groups. The art of "dialogue" would then be resuscitated and the ground be cleared for co-operation through conversational exploration and understanding.

It is interesting to note that the current emphasis on "dialogue" was promoted and publicized by a secular foundation, the Fund for the Republic, rather than by the churches and synagogues. Although The Jewish Theological Seminary, under the aegis of its Institute for Social and Religious Studies, had sponsored meetings between clergymen of different faiths for the past fifteen years, and thus could claim the patent of paternity, the range and reach of its audience was a limited one. The Fund for the Republic, stocked with adequate money and a national audience, was able to prod churchmen into dialogue with secularists in a historic meeting in New York in 1958.[22] The response to this and similar meetings, which have since been held in Chicago and Santa Barbara, has been amazing. Protestant and Catholic theologians and scholars, who had separately come to a state of mind receptive toward this kind of effort, are meeting together with increasing frequency and seriousness. The ground rules for religious dialogue, originally proposed by Robert McAfee Brown and printed simultaneously in *The Christian Century* and *The Commonweal*, were widely discussed in the daily press.[23]

A similar result has not yet arisen within American Judaism. Because the American synagogue has not yet cleared its throat of the encrustations of ethnicity, its voice is not often heard on either religious or social problems. No serious Jewish-Protestant dialogue, and certainly no Jewish-Catholic dialogue, has come to pass. The English-Jewish press, both denominational and a-denominational, could be instrumental in preparing American Jews for such possibilities. It could do a great deal to reawaken the

[22] *Religion in America* (New York: Meridian Books, 1959). This paperback contains the papers read at that confrontation.

[23] They are reprinted in *An American Dialogue*, co-authored by R. M. Brown and Gustave Weigel, S.J. (New York: Doubleday/Anchor Books, 1961).

theological dimension and social concern of American Judaism, and direct it outward—toward American society as a whole. It might even indicate that American Jews could co-operate with Protestants and Catholics on issues that are of transcendent concern to all three groups, such as the race problem in the United States, nuclear testing, and disarmament, *but from a specifically Jewish point of view.* Joint action, undertaken from different and even contradictory religious points of view, is both problem and prospect for the American Jewish community. The English-Jewish press could find no more important task than this to help it overcome its own aimlessness and irrelevance.

4 The Secular Uses of the Religious Press

ROBERT LEKACHMAN

WHAT is it reasonable to expect from the religious press as its contribution to a more enlightened life for the religiously indifferent? How does the religious press benefit a community wider than its own constituents? What has the community the right to expect from religious journals because of the objectives which religion—not society—professes to cherish? What have Protestant, Catholic, and Jewish periodicals to say to each other's readers?

Even to glance at questions of this order, it is essential to narrow the field of inquiry. Most religious periodicals are the trade or specialty organs of their denominations. This is to suggest that they concentrate upon the minutiae of church management, the problems of fund raising, the progress of religious education, and the activities of church officials, in very much the same way that magazines financed by philatelists and numismatists, or doctors and lawyers, properly emphasize specialized topics of concern only to their own constituencies. Without question, there is place for the many thousands of periodicals which fill the needs of the numerous church bodies now operating in the United States. No doubt also, their proliferation owes something to such well-examined sociological circumstances as inter- and intra-denominational rivalry, the inadequacies of the general press, and the contemporary lavishness with which Americans have been supporting the subsidiary activities of schools, universities, and churches. The instinct to publish must be very strong among humans.

I mention religious organs of this variety only as a preliminary to dismissing them from our discussion, for I am unable to see them as a proper object of either concern or interest for anyone but their own readers. What remains of the religious press is a relatively small number of periodicals whose mission is larger: either because it includes an effort to convert the community in general to the policies, if not the doctrine, of a faith; or attempts to identify the universal relevance of that faith; or endeavors to place contemporary political, social, and economic issues within a religious context. Such periodicals have a general interest and a general value, insofar as they approximate the achievement of any one of these objectives. At their best, these journals enable open-minded outsiders in the community to perceive grave public issues in a framework different from that of the secular magazine or newspaper.

My own reading leads me to include in this small group two Catholic organs, *America* and *The Commonweal*. Among Protestant journals, *The Christian Century* is by all odds the best-known journal of its kind, but *Christianity and Crisis* has attracted a small yet influential audience whose size is steadily growing. *Commentary*, sponsored and supported by the American Jewish Committee, is undoubtedly the most distinguished literary product that religious journalism has created. More recently a well-edited rival, *Midstream*, has been gracing the scene. These periodicals have achieved the greatest visibility, and accordingly they enjoy a measure of circulation beyond the various communities to which they directly address themselves. In some sense, at the least, they speak to all of American society.

These half-dozen journals are the best of their kind. But how good is "best"? What standard shall be applied? What criteria are appropriate? Let us apply this standard and see how we fare: a religious periodical contributes something to society when it comes closest to obeying E. M. Forster's injunction in *Howard's End*, ". . . only connect." By this criterion, a Catholic organ moves beyond special pleading for Catholics when it connects its views on aid to education, or the legalized abortion of deformed fetuses, with a conception of human nature and human objectives which encompasses the adherents of all religious and secular traditions. Or to take other instances, when a Protestant paper is able to place the civil rights movement within a strong religious tradition, or a Jewish periodical can relate the Supreme Court's prayer decision in *Engel v. Vitale* to Jewish political tradition, then the community in general benefits in understanding, even when it does not accept either the sources or the content of the conclusions that are reached.

Certainly secular society, to put the point in its most secular form, can benefit from the ethical expertise of Jewish and Christian practitioners, as it benefits from the advice of other specialists. Is it naïve to ask, is there a Christian or a Jewish foreign policy? Is there a disarmament program which stems from religious thought? Can religion extend some guidance to businessmen and union leaders in the conduct of their collective bargaining negotiations? Are there religious wage settlements? For that matter, are there religious guides to the conduct of businessmen? I remember very well a meeting some years ago in which a clergyman approached the question of the corporation's obligation to balance the conflicting claims of stockholders, employees, managers, customers, and suppliers by emphasizing the central importance of Christian love as an adjudicating principle. I wondered at the time, who should be loved, and how it was possible to love the stockholder more without loving the employee or the supplier less. Long ago, Nicholas Oresme, Bishop of Lisieux, observed that some occupations stain men's souls. Can religion guide the advertising man, the writer of cigarette commercials, or the tax lawyer? For that matter, can religion guide the passage of more equitable tax laws?

At this point in the argument it may seem that I have implied an unflattering answer to these queries and to the many others that are closely allied to them. Such has not been my intention, for some periodicals on some issues contribute substantially to public discussion and public understanding, in ways which draw upon their religious traditions. Such contributions are particularly notable in the instances of the two Catholic magazines before cited: both the rather moderate *America,* sponsored and edited by the Jesuit order, and the more liberal *Commonweal,* supported and controlled by Catholic laymen, speak out of their religious tradition instructively to the general public on a good many important issues. In recent years *America* has supported federal aid to parochial schools, the Kennedy Administration's "medicare" program, and the continuation of American policies of de-emphasis upon the population problems of underdeveloped societies. My point is illustrated by any one of these postures. When, for example, *America* not unexpectedly favors aid to parochial schools, it is able to place its case within a Catholic natural law doctrine which derives from the right of the parent—any parent—to control the education of his children, the proposition that the proper role of the state is that of the parent's delegate in offering the kind of education which the parent values for his child. Clearly the implications of *America*'s stand readily extend to Protestant, Jewish, and militantly atheist parents, as long as they possess firm notions of what a proper education comprises. Again, although most Protestant and Jewish groups (and almost all secularists) do not share Catholic opposition to artificial contraception, the Catholic position on this issue also derives from an understanding of the nature of man rather than from the simple self-interest of the Catholic Church. Even *America*'s much-criticized editorial of advice to Jews to moderate their separationist position on church-state issues was based upon a wider vision of society and communal relations which non-Catholics can also accept, or at least appreciate.

As for the Jewish periodicals, their role in the conversation among religious groups and between religious groups and society at large, which at its best the religious press fosters, is illustrated by a consideration of the very same issue of appropriate relationships between the state and the public schools. In its December 1962 issue, *Midstream,* an avowedly Zionist journal, carried as its two lead articles Rabbi Herbert Weiner's, "The Case for the Timorous Jew: Reflections on Church and State in America"; and Leo Pfeffer's, "Counterreflections on Church and State." Rabbi Weiner, the leader of a South Orange, New Jersey, congregation, argued quite plausibly for self-restraint by Jewish groups in their opposition to Christmas and Easter observances in the public schools, for willingness to compromise and avoid sharpening communal hostilities, and for recognition of the circumstance that American Jews are a perpetual minority in a Christian country. In its conclusions, if not in its arguments, Rabbi Weiner's position was not very far from *America*'s. Leo Pfeffer, general counsel of the American Jewish Congress and author of many articles and books on the constitutional issues which center upon the First Amendment, took sharp issue with Rabbi Weiner, both on the significance of the principles at stake and on the practical efficacy of Jewish moderation in historical communal controversies. What made both arguments especially interesting to an outsider was the effort of both writers to connect their analyses with a tradition greater in age and application than the American Constitution.

Rabbi Weiner appealed to "the," or at least to "an," Orthodox tradition in favor of closer union between state and church, and state and schools. Thus, he argued, Jewish tradition is not inevitably, or even usually, in favor of the strict separationist line taken by the American Jewish Congress and other Jewish organizations. For his part, Mr. Pfeffer called as witnesses the prophets Moses, Elijah, Jeremiah, Ezra, and Nehemiah. From their turbulent careers he drew the moral that good communal relations were never their objectives. If, Mr. Pfeffer went on, the high status of American Jewry made them reluctant to oppose wrong, then Jews lost their justification for survival. To a stranger to Jewish doctrine, the presence of these Jewish traditions adds a dimension to an argument which otherwise resembles the legalistic, constitutional controversies with which the last decade has familiarized anyone at all interested in church-state relations.

Christianity and Crisis projects the personalities of two remarkable individuals, John Bennett and Reinhold Niebuhr. The Niebuhrian vision of society emphasizes paradox, complexity, the mixture of human motives, and the inextricable confusion of good and evil which flaws all human choices. This highly sophisticated vision of the human situation in the nuclear age adds a tragic depth to the *Christianity and Crisis* discussions of foreign policy, disarmament, and the conditions of domestic political power. These are tortured times, not explicable by the simple lights of human rationality. Perhaps more than any other periodical, *Christianity and Crisis* has woven into its analyses of current affairs the knowledge that reason is limited. If the solutions to international and domestic dilemmas seem horribly difficult in the pages of this journal, it may only be because they are indeed horribly difficult.

I am grateful for what these religious journals give. I am grateful not only for the reasons that I have indicated, but also for the temperate tone and the civilized style that in general characterize these six magazines. As a group, they compare favorably in seemliness of expression with the better secular journals. One of their number, *Commentary,* ranks among the best-written magazines in the English-speaking world. But when all of this has been granted, the best religious periodicals still fail to connect their doctrines with much of contemporary life. At times the doctrines appear irrelevant to the issues they seek to elucidate. Sometimes important areas of contemporary life are neglected. Frequently religious journalism falls short of the precision and the specificity which influence in the contemporary world demands. Let us briefly consider each of these shortcomings.

RELEVANCE
AND IRRELEVANCE

The overriding issue of our time is the danger of thermonuclear war. If Jewish commentators have found anything in Judaism which assists understanding, they have not shared their insights with the readers of *Commentary* and *Midstream*. Catholic political doctrine does include a concept of a just war, which embodies a number of careful distinctions relating to the causes of war and the degrees of force which can appropriately be wielded by the just party. But at least as far as this doctrine is applied by Catholic journalists, it appears highly inadequate and only marginally relevant to the demands of the problem. It is unfair to expect a religious magazine to act as a foreign office, but it seems reasonable to expect of the specifically religious insight that it add something to the anguished discussion of the Herman Kahns, Albert Wohlstetters, and Samuel Huntingtons on the one side, and the H. Stuart Hugheses, Erich Fromms, and David Riesmans on the other. With the possible exception of *Christianity and Crisis*, none of these periodicals has done so. Rather, *Commentary* has served largely as an excellent forum for the reflections of such skilled polemicists as Sir Charles Snow, Hans Morgenthau, and H. Stuart Hughes.

Commentary is more generally an instance of religious irrelevance. Although the magazine always includes some articles and fiction of specifically Jewish concern, it is fair to say that the Jewish portion of the magazine is all too likely to fall into the categories either of nostalgic memoirs of persons and places, Jewish suburban sociology, or rarefied theology. *Commentary*'s widely noted symposium of younger Jewish intellectuals seemed to demonstrate, even at excessive length, that this group saw little connection between Judaism and their own lives and their own problems. Little of what *Commentary* publishes contradicts their conclusions. To take an issue at random, the October, 1962 number of *Commentary* contains as its lead article a piece on Katherine Anne Porter's *Ship of Fools*. Other essays include one of a series of economic pieces by David Bazelon, an article on "Neo-Freudianism & Erich Fromm," one of a series on John Dewey, and yet another analysis of "What the Russians Mean." Thus, by omission, the editors conveyed the message that the Jewish tradition has rather little relevance to contemporary issues of personality, economics, philosophy, and war and peace.

At this point I wish to avert misunderstanding. As an old admirer of *Commentary*, I look forward each month to its arrival, but it is with the same quality of expectation that I extend to the splendid English journal *Encounter*.

SCOPE

What occupies most people much of their time in their adult years is the work which they do. In a business community like the United States, the practitioners of such traditional occupations as farming, and the exponents of the learned professions of law, medicine, and letters, all are linked to a money economy whose values pervade economic life. I do not doubt that much of the skepticism of the irreligious about the scope of religion's impact on society is founded on the difficulty of identifying a specifically Christian or Jewish set of ethical guides to economic behavior. The great social encyclicals, "Rerum Novarum" and "Mater et Magistra," are noble in intention and constructive in social purpose. "Rerum Novarum" recognized the legitimate role of trade unions in a capitalistic society. Pope John's "Mater et Magistra" stresses the obligation of the rich nations of the world to succor their poorer neighbors. Unfortunately these are statements of attitudes, rather than guides to conduct.

But even this much is denied to Protestant and Jewish periodicals. No Protestant magazine is likely to derive much help from such solemn conclaves as the 1937 Oxford Conference on Church, Community, and State, whose 425 participants could unite only in requests to Christians to "bear witness to their faith within the existing economic order" and "test all economic institutions in the lights of their understanding of God's will." Even this thin brew was further diluted by warnings against any expectation of agreement among Christians where "technical factors predominate," or where opinions naturally differ because of disparate "economic, geographical, and historical circumstances." Where do they not? Nor could it be said that later efforts like the series of volumes on "Ethics and Economic Life," sponsored by the

Federal Council of Churches, advanced the case measurably. Therefore it is no occasion for astonishment that Protestant journals really have little that is helpful to say about the responsibilities of corporations, the proper limits and the appropriate goals of trade union activities, the personal ethics of business leaders, or the Protestant imperatives of public action in the economic order. It may be more accurate to say that the reflections of these journals on economic life differ only inconsequently from the remarks of *The New Republic*, the *New Leader*, and *The Reporter*. What Dr. Niebuhr writes on economic affairs is as comfortable in the pages of the *New Leader* as it is between the covers of his own *Christianity and Crisis*. Nor is the case different for Jewish periodicals. Ben Seligman, Oscar Gass, and David Bazelon might as readily have written their economic articles for other serious magazines as for *Commentary*.

The conclusion must be melancholy. In today's complex, technical world, mysteriously run by experts, the religious conceptions of ethical economic behavior which sufficed to guide men in simpler times are useless. More powerful substitute doctrines are nowhere to be seen.

PRECISION

Much of what I have to say under this heading I have already implied. To have force in the twentieth century, a recommendation must be specific and precise. It must incorporate a comprehension of the mechanism by which public and private instrumentalities move from one state of affairs to a preferred alternative. Thus traditional religious concern for the alleviation of poverty has little influence unless it is translatable into a series of meaningful programs which might include public encouragement to economic growth, well-defined policies of manpower retraining, exact arrangements for the relocation of families and industries, and specified tax encouragements to corporations for behavior which is in the public interest. And what is true of the alleviation of poverty is no less true of sophisticated approaches to the loftier issues of disarmament, foreign policy, and assistance to the poverty-stricken nations of Latin America, Africa, and Asia.

It is not that religious journalists have been unaware of the concrete challenges of these issues. But, by and large, they have been unsuccessful in one of two ways: they have failed to connect their religious vision to a sufficiently specific series of policies, or they have failed to demonstrate that an acceptable group of specific policies bears much connection with an identifying religious tradition. Perhaps this is only another way of saying that the assistance one is likely to get from the thoughtful economic comments of *America,* and *The Commonweal,* is either too general to be useful, or too like similar materials cast in a secular vein to incorporate any distinctive religious meanings. At their best, the religious journals supplement their secular rivals. At their worst, they are irrelevant.

A few words of conclusion will suffice to summarize my judgment of the general position of the religious journals. The best of them are good magazines, well worth reading. Some of the reasons for reading them do relate to their religious outlook upon issues of church and state, education, and public morality, for this outlook leads either to different conclusions or, at the least, to a different context for similar conclusions. Here the religious press contributes substantially to the public good. But in many respects the merits of the religious press are secular rather than religious. On domestic economic and political issues, as on the larger dilemmas of war and peace, even the best religious organs purvey very much the same menu as their secular associates. I am disappointed, finally, not in the literary standards of the best religious journals, but in their too-frequent incapacity to sound a clear religious note in the public dialogue.